Praise for
This Is the Day

"People have said that I'm frugal with my praise for others. Perhaps it's because I always expect those around me to give their best. Unfortunately, it's a fact that always giving our best is not in our nature. Rather, it's in our nature to take the easy way out. Being better than that and giving our best every day with a positive attitude is what makes us special. *This Is the Day* puts that notion in perspective. Tim Tebow gives the reader tools to make one's goals and dreams a reality. I admire Timmy as a friend and a philosopher of the game and life. He speaks from experience and from the heart."

—NICK SABAN, head football coach, University of Alabama

"I know it can be challenging to live with passion or to stay motivated. Through personal experience and heart-warming stories, my dear friend Tim Tebow shows you how. Learn the little and big changes you can make to transform your life and, in the exciting process, impact the world around you!"

—ROBIN ROBERTS, *Good Morning America*

"Often, we connect the phrase 'follow your dreams' into self-oriented goals we want to accomplish. Tim Tebow is all about living your dreams, but in a way that's meaningful—not just to become rich or famous or to look or feel good. *This Is the Day* is about becoming the person God created you to be and living a life filled with purpose."

—RICHARD PETTY, seven-time NASCAR
Championship winner

"No matter your gender, how old you are, your background, how much money you have (or don't) in the bank, there's something for everyone to be enjoyed in this book. Find practical ways to start living a life that means something instead of letting life keep you down."

—JAMIE FOXX, Oscar and Grammy Award winner

"I have followed Tim Tebow for many years and have always been so grateful for his strong, unswerving Christian testimony. His boldness and strength of character consistently inspire those around him, and his new book, *This Is the Day,* will continue to inspire many more. The Bible encourages us to make the most of the time we are given. With Jesus Christ at the center of our lives, there is no limit to what He can accomplish through us."

—FRANKLIN GRAHAM, president and CEO of Samaritan's
Purse and the BGEA

THIS IS
THE DAY

BOOKS BY TIM TEBOW

Through My Eyes

Shaken

Shaken Bible Study

Shaken Bible Study DVD

Know Who You Are. Live Like It Matters.

Shaken: Young Reader's Edition

NEW YORK TIMES BESTSELLER

TIM TEBOW

WITH **A. J. GREGORY**

THIS IS
THE DAY

Reclaim Your Dream. Ignite Your Passion.
Live Your Purpose.

WATERBROOK

THIS IS THE DAY

Copyright © 2018 by Timothy R. Tebow

All rights reserved.

Published in the United States by WaterBrook, an imprint of Random House, a division of Penguin Random House LLC.

WATERBROOK® and its deer colophon are registered trademarks of Penguin Random House LLC.

Paperback ISBN 978-0-525-65044-7

The Library of Congress has cataloged the hardcover edition as follows:
Names: Tebow, Tim, 1987– author.
Title: This is the day / Tim Tebow.
Description: First edition. | Colorado Springs, Colorado : WaterBrook Press, 2018. |
    Includes bibliographical references and index.
Identifiers: LCCN 2018011299 | ISBN 9780525650300 (hardcover : alk. paper) |
    ISBN 9780525650423 (ebook)
Subjects: LCSH: Christian life.
Classification: LCC BV4501.3 .T43 2018 | DDC 248.4—dc23
LC record available at https://lccn.loc.gov/2018011299

Printed in the United States of America on acid-free paper

waterbrookmultnomah.com

9 8 7 6 5 4 3 2 1

First Trade Paperback Edition

Interior book design by Karen Sherry

SPECIAL SALES
Most WaterBrook books are available at special quantity discounts when purchased in bulk by corporations, organizations, and special-interest groups. Custom imprinting or excerpting can also be done to fit special needs. For information, please email specialmarketscms@penguinrandomhouse.com.

To my greatest role models, who taught me that every day we can have purpose and meaning if we open our eyes to it. Thanks, Mom and Dad!

Contents

Introduction 1

1 This Is the Day Say "I Love You" 7

2 This Is the Day Get in the Game 25

3 This Is the Day Leave the Past Behind 45

4 This Is the Day Listen to the Right Voice 63

5 This Is the Day Believe in What Really Matters. . . . 75

6 This Is the Day Say Yes 91

7 This Is the Day Put in the Work 107

8 This Is the Day Open Your Eyes 127

9 This Is the Day Live with Open Hands 145

10 This Is the Day Flip the Script 161

11 This Is the Day Go Back to the Well. 179

12 This Is the Day Make It Count 193

Acknowledgments 209

Introduction

magine waking up each day fueled by a whisper: "This is the day." *A day for what?* you wonder. A day for change. A day that can be different, better than yesterday. A day that, even in the revolving door of responsibilities and to-dos, can be filled with more purpose and passion than you think possible.

Imagine when hearing the sound of the morning alarm, instead of groaning or slapping the snooze button, you awaken—mind, heart, and soul—to possibility. Something better. Something more.

You open your eyes, and before your feet hit the ground running, you pause. You choose not to be ruled by the tune of just getting by, not to allow what really matters to get swallowed up by the daily grind, and not to ignore what you really want out of life.

When I was a kid, my parents each had a unique way of waking up my siblings and me. The difference between Mom doing it and Dad doing it was pretty drastic. Mom would swing my bedroom door wide open and in her sweet voice sing the song based on Psalm 118:24: "This is the day that the Lord has made. We will rejoice and be glad in it." (If you went to church as a kid, you might remember singing this song.) Dad did things a little differently. He would rush in and shout in a deep voice, "Here we go! Are you alive, alert, awake, and enthusiastic?"

Differences aside, my parents made clear that this was the day to get out of bed and make it count.

This is the day that God has made. *This day. Right now.* Whatever moment you are breathing in, God made this day. Even when times are tough, something about this day is good. There's always a reason, however small, to find joy in this day. Sometimes we have to choose to look for it. Sometimes we have to ask God to help us find it.

God gives us today as a gift. He wants us to pursue it, not just for selfish ambition but to do something meaningful with it. To use it to grow, to love others well, to help someone, to pursue a dream He's put on our hearts. This is the day to live without fear of the unknown, without being chained by failure or what-ifs. This is the day to be willing to change, to be open, to believe, to hope. If we don't attack each day with this intentionality, it's almost like telling God, "Thanks, but no thanks."

How different would your day be if you lived out the words of Psalm 118:24? Think about it; really think about it.

Is there something you would change?

Is there someone you would reach out to?

Is there something you would need to give?

Is there something you would need to let go of?

I'm not saying putting this into practice is easy. Hard times are inevitable. Obstacles will come. Some battles are harder to fight than others. You may get knocked down, but you don't have to stay there. Each day you wake up, you have a chance to get unstuck, to step out of a comfortable routine that may be limiting your potential, and to fight for something that's important.

You were made not just to survive today but to thrive in it. I want to encourage you to stop putting off your dreams, your goals, and the purpose God has for you. It's time to become the person He has created you to be.

I wrote this book to get you to start thinking about what you can do, beginning today, to make a change. It doesn't have to be a grand gesture. Something as simple as recognizing divine moments, choosing to believe God over your doubts, taking action instead of complaining, and just opening your eyes and paying attention can impact your life and others' lives in powerful ways.

It's never too late. You're not too young. You're not too old. You can have purpose not only in your life but also in this day. There is always something you can do right now to improve yourself, to make an impact on someone or something else, or to create or enjoy a meaningful moment. Challenge yourself right now to begin to think about each day as an opportunity to crush it, to pursue the right things, to gain a better perspective, to step out of your comfort zone, and to go all in.

Whether you're a college grad needing the push to create and attack your five-year plan, a thirtysomething stuck in a job you hate, a single mom or dad struggling to get by and lacking joy, a career man or woman who feels a bit stuck, or an empty nester wondering what on earth you're going to do with your life, you can use the principles I offer in this book. It's time to uncover your God-given potential and start really living.

This is the day you can switch off autopilot and begin living with passion.

This is the day you can see what God sees.

This is the day you can overcome a bad habit or a character flaw.

This is the day that can bring you a step closer to your dreams and goals.

This is the day you can fight for what's right.

This is the day you can change someone's life for the better.

This is the day you can change your own life.

Life isn't just about *one* day. It's about *this* day.

1

Say "I Love You"

What a grand thing it is to be loved!
What a far grander thing it is to love!

—Victor Hugo

C lear blue skies to my left, the same on my right. I'm comfortable, planted on my seat watching a good movie. Like me, other passengers nearby are in their own worlds. Some are taking a nap. Others are glued to their electronic devices, fingers tapping rhythmically across keyboards.

And though I'm engrossed in the dramatic fight scene unfolding on my screen, I sense something. An inexplicable heaviness weighs down my heart.

A flight attendant stops to my right. "Can I get you something to drink, sir?" she asks with a smile.

I pull my headphones off. "No thank you, ma'am." Before I can park them back on my head, I hear commotion brewing in the background. I look back. Passengers are stirring in their seats, turning their heads to get a better view of something happening behind them. Loud gasps and concerned whispers explode. With a little over an hour of flight left before we're scheduled to land in Phoenix, Arizona, something potentially serious is unfolding.

About twenty-plus rows back, cabin crew members scurry about. As curious passengers start to stand up and lean over their rows, a flight attendant barks, "We need everyone to please stay seated. The aisles must be clear. I repeat, please remain seated."

There's too much commotion to figure out exactly what's going on. In the thick of the anxious buzz, I hear someone call out "Does anyone have an EpiPen?" as a flight attendant charges down the aisle toward the front of the plane.

A part of me feels drawn to the scene. *Maybe I can help. Maybe I can do something.* But I ignore the pull and put my headphones back on. *Someone probably had an allergic reaction or got sick or something. I don't want to be nosy. I'll let the flight attendants do their job.*

God nudges my heart. I can't escape the silent words that scream inside me. *You need to do something!*

Immediately, my mind spins with excuses for the next three seconds. *I'm really into this movie. And what can I do anyway? If I walk back there, I'll probably be more of a distraction than a help.* I think of more reasons to stay put. And do nothing.

Then a flight attendant appears in our cabin. "Is anyone here a doctor?" She looks calm, but the tone in her voice betrays alarm. When the passengers around me shake their heads, she hurries toward the back of the plane. I look at the people around me. Panic lines their faces. Concerned voices whisper back and forth.

"What's happening?"

"Why does she need a doctor?"

"Is someone hurt?"

My heart feels like lead. I'm totally unsettled now. I look back again and see a woman crying uncontrollably. There's movement in the aisle. But between flight attendants and a passenger or two doing something I can't quite make out, I still don't have a clue what's going on. The feeling of urgency is overwhelming. I can't just sit here and watch.

I stand up and walk toward the nearest flight attendant. "Excuse me, ma'am. I don't know what's going on back there. Is there anything I can do to help? Or maybe the woman back there, the one who's crying, maybe she would like me to pray with her?" Nodding, she forces a polite smile. I watch her leave. But she doesn't say a word to the woman who is obviously very upset.

I get the attention of another flight attendant and ask her the same thing. "Excuse me. I don't mean to bother you. But would you mind asking the woman back there if she'd like me to pray with her or encourage her or something?"

"Of course I will," she says.

A minute later, that flight attendant waves me over. As I make my way near the scene, I can see the soles of a man's shoes pointing toward the ceiling of the plane. He's lying prostrate in the aisle, not moving. A handful of people awkwardly positioned in the narrow space tower above the man. One of them is grasping his hand. "Sir, can you hear me? Squeeze my hand if you can hear me."

I notice a boy not far from the scene. Nine, maybe ten years old. I remember him passing me on the plane earlier. He was so excited to see me and wanted to say hello. The kid, now with eyes wide and tinged with fear, stares at the man on the floor. His dad is trying to cover his son's eyes.

My stomach churns. *Man. This kid does not need to see this.*

The obviously ill man's eyes are half open. Then they're closed and he looks to be unconscious. He's been stripped of some of his clothing, and blood drips down the side of his mouth. A female passenger kneels over him, pumping his chest with her bare hands. Looking for signs of life.

Just before I reach the inconsolable woman, she and a woman seated next to her lunge toward me, arms outstretched. Overcome with grief, the first woman doesn't say a word. She just slumps against my chest and cries. Teary eyed, the woman beside her whispers to me, "I've run out of words. You pray."

I wrap my arms around both women, who bury their faces in my shoulders. And as flight attendants hustle up and down the aisle and a passenger continues to perform CPR on the man on the floor, I pray. I pray for God's hand of mercy to cover him. I pray for a wall of protection over him. I pray for a miracle.

After I pray, the women tell me their names. Debbie is the wife of Boots, the sick man she thinks has gone into cardiac arrest. They've been married more than nineteen years. Karen, the woman with Debbie, is a coworker. Both hail from South Carolina. The three of us talk a bit before tears fall again.

"Boots was fine up until the last hour," Debbie says while trying to stifle a sob. "I could just tell something was wrong. I asked him if he wanted water or something, but he said no. Then he just stopped breathing." She shakes her head, unable to speak. Her shoulders tremble as she weeps. Karen and I pray while Debbie cries. It's a cycle we repeat many times over the final hour of flight. Talk. Pray. Cry. Talk. Pray. Cry.

At some point, someone suddenly yells, "Stand clear!" The paddles of a defibrillator slap down on Boots's bare chest. He bucks violently and thuds back on the ground, motionless.

"Nothing," the person holding the paddles mutters. "Again."

The defibrillator discharges and the body heaves. "I think I got a pulse!"

Hope speaks.

As we descend toward the runway, I hold Debbie and Karen tight. With so much crying and praying and chaos, I barely feel the wheels touch down on the tarmac. The hour I was with Debbie flew by in what felt like minutes.

Approaching sirens wail as we taxi. As the passengers disembark the plane in haste, flight attendants quickly scramble to evacuate Boots out the rear of the plane. Someone tells me I can't stay with Debbie and must go. As I leave, she tries to squeeze her way into the aisle between flight attendants so she can accompany her husband in the ambulance that's just arrived. "No," Debbie is told. "I'm sorry, but you can't go out this way. You must exit the plane out the front. It's standard procedure."

We all deplane and soon after I meet up with Debbie and Karen. I offer to take them to the car that's waiting for me and to find their checked luggage. Debbie clutches her handbag with trembling hands and can barely stand. She tries to explain what her suitcase looks like. I slide an arm around Debbie's waist to support her, while still holding on to her husband's blood-stained clothing, everyone's carry-on bags by my feet. Lost in a world that has just fallen apart, Debbie clings to the words *I think I got a pulse.*

The next hour or two are a blur. A police officer, who looks like he's seen plenty of hard years on the job, tells me which hospital they're taking Boots to. He offers to escort us there. With all our luggage finally in hand, Debbie, Karen, and I drive off. We race down the highway, the ride filled with tears and hopeful prayers. After navigating our way to the emergency room and parking right behind the police officer's car with flashing lights, we

> It's tough to witness someone's world collapse before her eyes.

are directed into a room to wait. More tears. More prayers. Finally, a doctor enters and says to Debbie, "I'm sorry for your loss."

Debbie turns white. She hadn't realized her husband had died. Hearing the painful truth unsteadies her balance. Her knees buckle and she crashes into my arms. The cop shakes his head and rests his hand on her shoulder. He whispers, "I am so sorry your husband passed." I'll never forget his kindness. He stayed with us for hours afterward, even while I accompanied Debbie to identify her husband's body in another cold hospital room.

It's tough to witness someone's world collapse before her eyes. And, telling. These moments, shocking, heart breaking, and gut wrenching, remind me that life is fragile. And it can be cut tragically short. We don't know how much time we have on earth. We don't know how many days we have to spend with loved ones, to say what we want to say, to show our appreciation, to make sure they know we love them.

Later, Debbie told me that a month before her husband passed away, they were watching a movie at home. She felt in her heart a strong urge to tell him something. So Debbie turned to Boots. As she looked in his face, she saw a good man. A man determined to live, to not let life just happen to him. Here was a Vietnam vet who during the war had begged God to let him return home safely. And when he touched down on American soil, mourning the loss of his buddies in uniform who did not, Boots made some choices.

Debbie remembers him saying, "The men in my family have a history of dying young, but I can't let that stop me from living now. I want to do things. I want to see things. I want to enjoy life." In fact, before the two got married he said, "I hope you love to travel. When I was growing up, my parents promised each other they would start traveling once they retired. When Dad finally did, he took my mom on one cruise. Soon after, my father had a stroke and died."

Boots vowed to himself and his new wife that he wasn't going to wait to do what he'd always wanted to do. While he wasn't the kind of guy to show romantic love through bouquets of roses or whispering sweet nothings into his wife's ear, he showed Debbie his love through action. Like how he had been her rock, supportive, present, and encouraging, when she battled leukemia. The calm in her storm, no matter how bad things got, Boots would always put a smile on his face and tell his beloved wife, "Don't you worry. We're going to be just fine."

So, as Debbie sat on that couch looking into the face of a man who meant the world to her, she said, "Boots, if I haven't told you lately, thank you for everything you've done for me. I appreciate you more than you know. I love you so much."

A month later, her rock was gone.

———

Life is a gift. Each day is precious—and at times fleeting. Pain and tragedy are constants in our time on earth. When I started writing this book, a string of hurricanes unleashed incredible damage. These storms destroyed communities, cities, and even entire countries. Hurricane Harvey killed an estimated eighty people and displaced more than one million in a path of destruction stretching more than three hundred miles. Hurricane Irma barreled in on Harvey's heels, ravaging many Caribbean islands, including Barbuda, which it almost completely wiped out, as well as my home state of Florida. More storms followed, like Hurricane Maria, which left the entire island of Puerto Rico without power and water for months.

Disasters don't occur just in nature. As I was writing this chapter in October 2017, a man rained gunfire on a country music concert in Las

Vegas, killing fifty-eight people and injuring five hundred others. There were other shootings in churches and schools, which claimed many lives, including children.

Things happen that we do not understand. Sometimes lives are lost, taken away from us too soon. This is sad and yet very real. We can't control the path or the magnitude of whatever storms or disasters come our way. We can't anticipate our losses. And we can't hold on to the promise of tomorrow.

So what's something we *can* do? We can this day celebrate the ones we love. We can create special moments with them. We can say "I love you."

CHECK YOURSELF

When I met Debbie, she reminded me of something I'd been working on: creating meaningful moments with my family and my friends. I want to be intentional not only in telling them I love them but also in showing them.

A few years ago, I wrote down five life goals:

1. Show Jesus.
2. Fight for those who can't fight for themselves.
3. Take care of the people I love with resources, finances, and blessings.
4. Be a protector of people.
5. Pursue my dreams.

For me, part of what it means to take care of the people I love is to make memories with my family. This really started to hit home recently, especially with my parents getting older. I began to realize that I wasn't going to have them around forever.

I've always appreciated my family, but I was awakening to how truly precious it is to spend time with Mom and Dad, as well as my siblings and my nieces and nephews. Thing is, unless I strove to make it happen, it wouldn't. Because let's be real: life always gets in the way. They're busy. I'm busy. We're all busy, right?

Like with everything I do, I started getting aggressive with scheduling time for the family. It's tough to get together with everyone when we live in different states and even in different parts of the world. I didn't let that stand in my way. I started planning trips. I scheduled a siblings-only vacation in Mexico. The entire family reunited for both Thanksgiving and Christmas. We went to the Bahamas one summer. In December, while working on this book, I went to Dubai and several surrounding countries with my parents for ministry opportunities. And in January 2018, I arranged a trip for the entire family to Honolulu because I knew that Dad, a history buff, would enjoy visiting Pearl Harbor and others would appreciate the Hawaiian paradise.

Sometimes we just need a healthy reminder of what's important— *people.*

Look, you don't have to spend thousands of dollars and whisk your family or friends away to show them you care. It's about setting the right priorities. Twenty years from now, what's going to matter more: Taking your mom out to dinner or crossing off something on your to-do list? Spending an afternoon with your kids at the park or doing the laundry? Talking to your grandmother over tea or going to the movies with friends you see all the time?

I'm not saying to-do lists or housework or movies are bad things or things we should stop doing. But sometimes we just need a healthy reminder of what's important—*people.* It always comes down to people. The ones we love. The ones who won't be around forever. The ones who make us smile and laugh, as well as know how to push our buttons.

SHOWING MY DAD THE LOVE

In the spring of 2016, my parents attended the annual Tim Tebow Foundation (TTF) gala, when a good friend of ours noticed Dad's hands were shaking. This man recommended a renowned specialist who could diagnose the illness.

I'll never forget getting the phone call from my dad and mom. I was in a hotel room in Atlanta, getting ready to start taping the TV show *Home Free*. When my parents opened the conversation by saying, "Timmy, we have something to tell you," I just knew something was wrong. When I heard the word *Dad* coupled with *Parkinson's disease,* the shock hit me so hard the room started to spin.

Dad has Parkinson's?

I didn't sleep at all that night. When morning came, I was covered in hives. For me, emotional stress manifests in a physical way.

I've since had time to process the news and have tried to support Dad as much as I can. He is my rock. Seeing him fight through the disease and continue to live each day with purpose and meaning is so inspiring. I have never seen him give up or quit. Even today, he is still working tirelessly as a missionary serving the people of the Philippines and surrounding countries. What an example! Ever since Dad got sick, spending time with him has been more of a priority than ever before.

Honestly, if my father weren't around, I doubt I would have had the courage to pursue my baseball dream. He encourages and believes in me so much that he makes me believe in myself so much more!

Since I was a little boy, he's always been my biggest cheerleader. I'll never forget one Little League T-ball game I played when I was four. Even as a tot, I was a fierce competitor. Win or die—that already was my motto. I remember our coach gathering the team in a huddle before the start of the game. Sweat dripped down the sides of my face as the merciless Florida sun beat down. One of my four-year-old teammates near me smashed his cleat over an anthill. Another squinted lazily at the blazing sky. I waited with bated breath for Coach's words of inspiration that were sure to lead our team into the glory of victory.

"Remember, guys," our fearless leader said with a wide smile, "it doesn't matter if you win or lose. This is about fun. So have a good time out there!"

As my teammates cheered and high-fived each other, my jaw dropped. *Fun? What is he talking about?* My family had just moved back from the Philippines, and this was my first time playing an American sport that actually counted. I mean, I was on a team that had a name. I was wearing a jersey with a number that I'd chosen. We were playing on an official field with a scoreboard. To me this was more than just fun. This was real. It meant something.

I piped up, hoping to throw some mature four-year-old wisdom the man's way. "No, Coach. It's *only* about winning. Because *that's* when you have fun!"

Coach didn't say a word. His eyes just bulged out of his head. "Wait right here, son," he said just before walking away toward the stands where my father sat. Looking back, I'm pretty sure he was thinking something along the lines of *Who does this punk kid think he is?*

As I heard Coach say something like "I think we have a problem with your son" and saw him motion to my father to follow him, my heart sank. I started to regret what I'd said. Look, I didn't want to get in trouble. I just wanted to play ball. After the two conversed, Dad made his way toward me.

Sheepish, I stared at the ground as Dad squatted in front of me. "Timmy?" he said, lifting my chin up with his hand.

"Yes, Dad?"

"It's okay, bud. The coach just doesn't understand."

That was Dad for you! See, my father knew me. He loved me. He believed in me. And he never let me forget it. When I made the decision to play baseball again, Dad never wavered in his support. When some questioned my motives and others told me I was too old to even consider this an option, Dad told me, "If this is something you want to do for the next few years, do it."

I can't tell you how many times he's called and said, "I believe you can make it. And if not, I will still love you and support you and believe in you." When I was playing with the Columbia Fireflies and found myself in a hitting slump, he'd text something like, "I pray that you go 5 for 5 tomorrow. And I love you whatever happens." And if my slump continued in the next game, he'd send another message: "I pray you go 5 for 5 tomorrow, and I love you!"

Dad also knew well the spiritual battle I was going through. I wasn't just fighting to get three hits or to hammer a home run; I was fighting against the Enemy's whispers—his lies that I was wasting my time on a pipe dream. Dad's spiritual support through his relentless prayers meant the world to me—it still does and always will! I'm so grateful for him, and I cherish the moments we spend together.

Now, I'm not going to pretend we have this perfect relationship. As amazing as Dad is, he's still a human being. And so am I. When Dad is visiting me in the States or staying at my house, he'll spend every waking moment with me. I'm not exaggerating. When I was playing for the Port St. Lucie Mets, he came to a few games. He'd hang around from the time I started signing autographs before practice until the game was over, and then we'd get something to eat before the night was over and hang out more until we said good night.

Here's the thing: I love Dad more than words can say. But sometimes a guy needs some space. We all do. There are times after hanging out together for sixteen hours straight that I start to feel a bit crowded. I'm not suffocating, by any means. All I need is a little breathing room.

You can probably relate, if not with a parent, then with another person who is close to you, like a spouse, a sibling, or a friend. Sometimes the ones we love can drive us nuts. We love these people. We enjoy spending time with them. We may think they are the coolest people on the planet. But sometimes they can do things or say things that get on our nerves, even just a little.

For me, when I'm tempted to let the little things in my relationships grow into big things, I force myself to back down. When I'm with sweet Dad and I start feeling a bit crowded, I just remember that one day I'm going to long for this moment to be with him. One day I'm going to wish he were with me.

So, I enjoy every minute with him, Mom, and everyone in my life—even when they keep asking when I'm going to get married.

Unplanned Detours

I've also learned that sometimes showing love means doing things that may seem inconvenient or initially may not make sense.

In July 2016, I took a group of people, including a few of our TTF donors, some of our staff, my brother Robby, and others to the Philippines. I had a sense of urgency about this trip that I couldn't fully explain or understand at the time. In fact, I had planned it at the last minute, only ten days before we flew out of the United States.

After arriving in the Philippines, our team met up with some folks from Dad's ministry organization. We visited his orphanage and my hospital and worked together to share the gospel in different places. I was looking forward to speaking in some of the prisons in Manila, but that didn't work out. As disappointed as I was, I remember thinking, *It's okay. God has a plan. And the rest of our trip is going to be awesome.*

It was. Every person experienced powerful, life-changing moments. It was humbling and uplifting to see God work in this special place. On our last night, I had the opportunity to speak at one of our orphanages. I talked about Dad and the millions of people whose lives have been influenced through his ministry. These people are different, better, because of what he has allowed God to do through him. I can't tell you how awesome this is to see as his son. (Now I'm tearing up just thinking about it.) The kids at the orphanage put on a talent show for us, a traditional custom. It was sweet and heartwarming. It reminded me of all the talent shows my siblings and I had to do when we were kids growing up in this country.

The night before we were scheduled to fly back to the States, one of our donors offered to host us at a hotel near the airport in Manila. After hugging and saying goodbye to Dad and all the people he serves with, I got into a van for the drive to the city.

For some reason I felt unusually sad. Quiet. While the van buzzed with chatter from people recounting amazing moments on this trip, I didn't say much. I'd had a great time, and it was so special to hang with my dad, whom I don't often get to see. But something was bothering me. Something didn't feel right about leaving. I felt God tugging on my heart: *Stay. You have more to do here.*

My initial thought was definitely not enthusiastic. I started listing in my mind all the reasons this thought was crazy. The flights, my schedule—all these things and more had already been planned out. I had events back home to attend. Others were counting on me. In fact, in a few weeks I'd announce my decision to pursue baseball and put on a showcase for Major League

Baseball scouts and media. Arrangements had been made. And yet, the more excuses I had, the stronger the pull.

You need to be with your dad. He is fighting for his life. He needs you.

Just before we arrived for the meeting with the donors, I turned to Anne, who has worked as my assistant for several years. "I think I need to stay," I told her.

Her eyes widened. "Are you serious?"

I nodded. Others with us overheard our brief conversation and were taken aback by the sudden decision. "Why?" "What's going on?" "Is everything okay?"

After a couple of deep breaths, Anne replied, "Okay, we'll make it happen." And she did!

My life moves at a very fast pace with a nonstop, hectic schedule—sometimes even travel to other countries. I'm usually hopping from an event on one side of the US to the opposite coast for an event or baseball training or any number of things. At times, Anne joins me on my travels to help coordinate the scheduling and the many details that come with the different things I do.

> Tomorrow is not promised. Make time and show someone you care.

The next day our team from TTF headed to the airport to catch a flight back home. I stayed behind. I phoned a friend of Dad's, who offered to drive me to the school where my father was serving. When we got there, Dad's back was turned toward me. I crept up behind him and gave him a bear hug.

His eyes went wide. "Timmy, is everything okay?"

"Yeah, Dad, everything is great. I just felt like I had to be with you for a couple more days."

My father didn't say a word. Tears dripped from his eyes.

During the next few days, I was blessed to—get this—have the opportunity to speak at several different prisons where hundreds of inmates made the decision to trust in Jesus. That time led to our meeting wonderful people who opened doors so Dad could further his ministry serving the people in the Philippines.

Most of all, I got to enjoy special moments with my father, moments I will treasure for the rest of my life. We talked. We prayed. He encouraged me in my pursuit of baseball. I told him how much I love and appreciate him.

Tomorrow is not promised. Make time and show someone you care. Tell a loved one that you are grateful for his support. Encourage a sibling to chase after the dream she's put on the back burner. Say yes to making memories, even if it means rearranging a carefully planned morning. And whether in word or deed, always choose to say "I love you."

MAKE THIS YOUR DAY

People matter more than schedules, more than lists, and more than tasks. We know this, but what does it really mean? How do we live this out? Showing love to others may mean a simple shift of your priorities.

Think about what matters most. Choose the more important things over the lesser ones. Balance busy calendars with meaningful moments. Call a friend and let him know you're thinking about him. Unplug the phones, gadgets, and devices, and be more present with a friend, spouse, parent, or child.

Do you find yourself taking from others or investing in them?

2

THIS IS THE DAY

Get in the Game

Twenty years from now you will be more disappointed by the things that you didn't do than by the ones you did do. So throw off the bowlines. Sail away from the safe harbor. Catch the trade winds in your sails. Explore. Dream. Discover.

—Anonymous

It was a come-to-Jesus moment. For my future, at least. In early 2015, around a long conference table sat those people I trusted with decisions for my career and in life, including agents and family members. We were discussing the next steps in my professional journey. It had been eighteen months since an NFL team had asked me if I'd play quarterback for them. So, what next?

I mentioned in my second book, *Shaken,* that at the time, a bunch of different offers were presented. There were opportunities to play different positions other than quarterback in the NFL. I also had offers to play in the Canadian League. Television prospects were on the table too. A lot of good things that I was truly grateful for.

It's funny; every agent in that room had a plan for my life. They seemed very confident in knowing what was good for me. With much persuasion, they shot out a list of selling points.

"If you play for such-and-such team, you could make this much money, and here is what the next five years of your life could look like."

"If you say yes to this television opportunity, your brand could explode and take you in such-and-such direction."

My agents took into account the money, the fame, and the power that would come but didn't consider one thing: my passion, what burned a fire in my heart.

I listened to idea after idea, pitch after pitch, and offer after offer. These weren't things I necessarily didn't want to do. There was just something I wanted to do more—and now. So I rerouted the conversation in an entirely different direction.

"What about baseball?"

You could hear a pin drop. The next few seconds of awkward silence were almost painful.

I said something like, "Look, I've loved playing ball since I was a kid, and most of you know it was one of my hardest decisions ever to give it up to play football. You probably think I'm crazy, but maybe, just maybe, this is something that could be real."

Everyone started talking at once. Opinions started flying around, phrased in polite ways.

One said, "Are you sure about this?"

Another, "Have you thought about how hard it could be?"

I had a feeling most were sugarcoating what was really on their minds. "Just tell me the truth," I said. "What do you really think?"

While those closest to me lent positive support, I also heard some not-so-positive thoughts from others. Things like "It's bad for your brand" and "You're too old." Someone suggested it might work but only if I did it with a reality TV show.

I'm sure my agents wondered why someone who was voted a few years earlier as one of the most trusted and most popular athletes in America and who became the fifth best-selling NFL player of sports merchandise would back his way down to the low-end minor leagues in a sport he hadn't played since high school. If memory serves me right, someone even asked, "Why would you humiliate yourself like that?"

What can I say? It mattered more what was in my heart than what others wanted me to do. I wanted to try and play baseball. Was it crazy? Maybe. Was it a long shot? Maybe. Was it in my best interest? Maybe. Maybe not. But it didn't matter.

As it turned out, one of the top agents in baseball, Brodie Van Wagenen, was right down the hall. Talk about perfect timing. Someone brought him in. It might sound strange to say, but when this dude walked into that conference room, he had a glow about him. I immediately liked him. In the end, my instinct was right. Today he is not only my agent; he is also a friend.

I don't remember exactly how I started that first conversation. I just wanted to communicate my passion for baseball. I wanted Brodie to realize that this pursuit wasn't a half-hearted effort or something I'd just drummed up to fill my time. I remember saying, "Brodie, just do me a favor and watch me play. If you like what you see, if you spot some potential, great. If you don't like what you see and decide I can't play, that's okay too. Just give me a chance. Watch me play."

> I didn't know what the outcome would be, but I was committed to the journey.

Brodie nodded with a smile and said, "Okay, Tim. I'm in."

I got so psyched in that moment. Brodie didn't see the idea as an empty glass. He saw a drop of water in there. A tiny drop, maybe. Still, it was something.

Let me explain my mind-set at the time. Whenever I would think about the dream of baseball, I'd get excited. The kind of excitement that runs deep in the pit of a soul. It wasn't about the money. I'd make practically nothing to start, and with everything I wouldn't be able to do by making this commitment, I'd actually lose money. It wasn't about the glamour. It would be a long and hard road to potential success. It also wasn't about the fame of being a baseball player. I had long ago determined that my identity is not centered on being a professional athlete but in who I am in Jesus.

Simply put, I love the game of baseball. Always have. In the middle of my senior year in high school, I had to make a choice between playing baseball or football. And like I said earlier, it was a painful choice.

Before I told everyone in that conference room I wanted to pursue this dream, just like I do in all things, I had prayed about the decision. I can't tell you I had full assurance that this was exactly something God wanted me to do. Then again, I've never had that feeling about a lot of things. There might be a ton of Christians out there who feel that God tells them exactly what to do. I'm not one of them. I know my ultimate purpose in life is to love God and love others. I also believe I can do that while I pursue other things I'm passionate about, like sports.

In praying and seeking counsel from those I trusted, I made the decision. I didn't know what the outcome would be, but I was committed to the journey.

NEXT STEPS

When the meeting was over, Brodie set up a time for me to play ball with several Cuban professionals in Florida. Some of them had just signed multi-million-dollar contracts. Others were preparing for their own pro workouts.

It was the first time I had competed with a baseball bat in my hand since my team lost the semifinals in the Florida state tournament when I was a junior in high school. My goal was to see how I felt getting coached and working drills for the first time in ten-plus years. Would I be as excited as I thought? Or would I realize the sport wasn't something I wanted to pursue?

I showed up at a ballpark in Boca Raton with my brother Robby and my friend Brad. Brodie pulled up alongside us in a rental car. Funny, I remember not having one piece of baseball gear to wear or play with. Hey, I'd been playing football for the last decade! I didn't own a single pair of baseball pants, sliding shorts, or anything.

Brodie opened the trunk of his car and started pulling out some clothes in different sizes, not knowing what would fit. I changed right there in the parking lot. Then I checked out the stockpile of bats, gloves, and cleats. The bat I chose was pretty special. After testing it out with a few swings, Brodie mentioned it was previously used by Major League Baseball (MLB) multi-all-star player Ryan Zimmerman. It was pretty cool knowing this heavy piece of lumber was once in the hands of an amazing baseball player.

The minute I stepped into the cage and slipped this bat into my hands, it felt like no time had passed. I swung so hard and so many times, blood seeped through my gloves. I remember Brodie staring at my hands after the cage work.

"How are you doing, buddy?" he asked, concerned.

I looked at him stone faced. "I'm fine."

"No, seriously, Timmy. You're taking a lot of swings. If your hands are bothering you and you need a break, it's okay."

I was ready to shut this conversation down. "I'm fine, man. Let's go." By the time the practice ended a few hours later, my gloves were drenched with sweat and blood from the multiple blisters that had popped. Who cared? I was there to show Brodie what I was capable of. I was going to do whatever it took to make him see my commitment to this game.

When it was time to hit the field for live pitching, I felt good. I wasn't nervous. I was having fun and getting more excited about this prospect with each passing minute. I felt relaxed at the plate, my muscles loosened from the drills. My hands gripped the bat lightly as I took a few practice swings. I stared at each pitcher, waiting for him to whirl and fire the ball toward me. With my weight shifted onto my back leg, I swung. The crack of the bat echoed in my ear as the ball sailed away over left field.

I love the challenge of baseball. It's one of the hardest sports to play. Think about it. As a ball player, the goal is to hit the ball with the "sweet spot" of the bat, which results in the maximum energy delivered to the ball with little or no vibration in your hands. Then the ball will travel its farthest—hello, home runs! Now imagine how hard this is. Using a round bat, you have to make contact with a five-ounce round ball traveling at ninety-plus miles per hour within one-eighth inch of the sweet spot. And it gets even more complicated! Once a pitcher releases his pitch, it takes about four hundred milliseconds, or four-tenths of a second, for the ball to reach the batter. In that minuscule amount of time, the batter must judge the ball's speed and location, determine whether or not to swing, and if so, where to hit the ball on the field. That's definitely not the easiest thing in the world to do, especially after not playing baseball for ten years.

I was doing really well, making good contact and showing power. With every crack of the bat, my passion grew deeper. *This wasn't just wishful thinking. I just might be able to do this.* What happened next was, well, confusing.

I was on deck right before my fourth or fifth at bat, when my brother Robby called out to me through the fence.

"Chip Kelly is trying to reach you," Robby said. "He wants you to try out to be quarterback."

Time froze. My heart thumped wildly. On one hand, I was pumped. If there was one team in the NFL I was going to get excited about, it was the Philadelphia Eagles. I liked their system and their up-tempo offense. On the other hand, what about baseball?

I remember standing on deck, half hearing the chatter in the dugout, half staring at Robby's wide-eyed face. My mind raced with this new twist. *Why now, God? I was getting more comfortable with the idea of pursuing baseball. Lord, do You want me to keep playing football? No one calls in over a year and a half, and as I'm literally taking a step forward to do something different, a position as a quarterback opens for me? Is this a sign to give up this new dream?* It didn't make sense. And it was frustrating. Why would God open two doors at the same time?

I prayed about the decision and, well, you know which door I walked through. And you know how that ended.

I've learned that when you start chasing the desires of your heart, most times one of two things will happen. Either God will grant them or He will change your desires.

DRAWING BOARD

Baseball was waiting for me after I was released from the Eagles. Back to training in secret. I went to pretty significant lengths to work on my craft without anyone knowing, besides those closest to me and Brodie. I spent most of the spring and summer of 2016 in Arizona training with talented coaches to see if I could get into position to put on a scouting showcase. That was the only plan at that point—train, get better.

At one point in March or April, when word started leaking out within a small baseball community, an old high school coach came out to watch me practice. He brought along a friend I didn't recognize. Right in the middle of my workout, this guy came over and told me he was a longtime professional scout for an MLB team. Then he said, "Listen, Tim. I know I promised I wouldn't give myself away, but if I don't tell my team about seeing someone with power and bat speed, I'll get fired."

I was flattered, of course. But more than anything, it was a key moment in affirming my dream. I needed feedback from professionals, even though I also needed to keep this pursuit secret. The plan intensified then. Brodie and I had to think through two options: whether to make myself available for the June 16 MLB draft or wait and stay underground to train and present the best version of myself for a showcase.

> I just needed to keep training. Bloody hands and all.

I decided to keep training. We tentatively scheduled a workout for the end of August to be performed in front of a number of MLB scouts. The only roadblock would be getting drafted before then. I called in a favor and spoke to someone at that one interested MLB team. "I'm just not ready yet," I told them. "I'm still figuring out my next steps."

I just needed to keep training. Bloody hands and all.

Didn't Expect That to Happen

In one of my last hitting practices, two days before my workout in front of prospective MLB teams, I hit the field ready for some live pitching. Standing at the plate, I faced a pitcher who came out to compete.

In less than forty-eight hours, I'd be under a proverbial microscope. More than forty-five scouts from twenty-eight teams, in addition to a circus of media members, about fifty from fourteen major networks, would probe my every move. Most, I'd heard, were approaching my workout with skepticism, calling it a joke and a sideshow.

Even before the first pitch was thrown out, I knew I wanted to make a statement. Power. That's all I could think about. Power. I swung hard. Violently hard. As soon as the bat flew over my shoulder, it felt like a knife sliced into my right oblique. As the pain seared through my side, I felt embarrassed and angry with myself. *What were you thinking? Why didn't you warm up more? The workout is only days away!* To be fair, baseball was still fairly new to me. I was getting used to the differences in mechanics between playing football and this new sport. My swing is a lot smoother than those early days, but it was definitely something I had to finesse at the time.

Brodie; my trainer, Ian Danney; and one of my coaches, Chad Moeller, a guy I appreciate for the time and work he invested in me, sat near the fence. Instead of telling them I probably tore my oblique muscle, I took a few more practice swings. By then, the pain was crippling. I plunked the bat on the ground and walked toward them.

"Y'all are not going to like this," I said, while Ian, Brodie, and others looked at me funny. "I hurt my side."

Those who know me well, particularly trainers and coaches, know that if I say I hurt myself, I've hurt myself badly. I rarely let an injury, pain, or soreness stop me from doing what I need to do. Let me put it this way. In high school I played in a game with a broken leg. In college I played with a broken hand. When I was playing in the NFL, I played with broken ribs.

Ian's face fell. "Oh shoot," he said, though he may have used a more colorful word instead. He started to work on my oblique, assessing the damage I'd done.

"How bad is it?" Brodie asked, as Ian began to work his magic kneading the injured area.

Ian's face looked grim. "Pretty bad," he replied, to everyone's disappointment, mainly mine. "The right oblique is definitely torn."

Here are some fun facts for you: Oblique muscles connect the pelvis to the torso. Healthy obliques are important to most athletes but specifically to ball players because these muscles are responsible for taking the power generated from the pelvis to the arms to create the swing and control the follow-through. A compromised oblique equals a compromised swing.

There was nothing I could do but submit to Ian's expertise. He worked on me round the clock. While he couldn't fix me, he got the damaged area to the point where the muscles around it started to relax. It wasn't a pain-free environment, but it meant that with enough rest and more of Ian's magic, I'd be able to get through the workout. We banked on the adrenaline rush during my performance to override the pain.

SHOWTIME

Finally, the day came. On Tuesday, August 30, 2016, my brother Robby, my dad, Ian, my coaches, and my agent arrived at 9 a.m. at the University of Southern California's Dedeaux Field. Those invited to the two-hour workout had received a press release detailing the course of the event. I'd start by running the sixty, then field some grounders and fly balls and throw to bases. Then I'd get in some batting practice and finally face live pitching by two former professional pitchers.

I hadn't slept well, but knowing so many people were praying for me helped. I remember walking the field with Robby and my dad the day before, figuring out where I was going to run the sixty. The ballpark was empty, quiet. With my recent injury and the pressure that was weighing heavy on me from this showcase, none of us were overly chatty. Robby and Dad, always my two biggest supporters, threw in encouraging bits while I focused on my surroundings.

My eyes fixed on the field where, mitt in hand, I'd field balls. I stared into the batter's box, picturing myself swinging just right and seeing the ball rocket out of the park. I didn't know how the workout would go. I just knew at this point, I'd prepared as best as I could, working and training hard. I'd done the best I knew how, and while I was far from a finished product, I just wanted to show some talent, a reason for these baseball pros to give me a chance.

Back at the workout. I breathed deeply, inhaling the scent of freshly mowed grass. I set up with Robby, Dad, and others on the backfield, away from members of the media, scouts, and others who would arrive soon at the ballpark.

Decked out in Adidas swag, I warmed up in a light jog and stretched out my shoulders. Robby cheered me on as he always does in big moments like these. Dad did too. He kept quoting Scripture and telling me, "God's got this." I couldn't help but notice how nervous Dad was. I was already nervous, and seeing him on edge squeezed my bundle of nerves a little bit tighter. Hey, I'd be a machine if I wasn't nervous. This was a live workout. Live! No takes. No redos. I was trying to do something I hadn't done since high school in front of, essentially, the world.

As the workout drew near, people started filing in. Aside from the scouts, there was a volume of media that was unheard of in the context of a baseball showcase of this magnitude. A convoy of media trucks from different networks were parked outside, and equal numbers of press and scouts piled into the park. Major networks were represented, including CNN, the *New York Times,* the MLB Network, and the NFL Network.

Also present were some acquaintances and agents I hadn't seen or talked to in a year or so. It's funny. I've noticed that most people want to be there for you in big moments. But few are with you during the preparation, the training, the hard work it takes to get there. Everyone loves to show up at the big games, the press conferences, the championship playoffs, but most of those same people aren't with you when you're exhausted and needing to push yourself through a workout or when it's midnight and your trainer is trying to work your body out of pain, soreness, or injury. It's so important to be supported and to support others in the little things. Be present behind the scenes. Show up when the work is happening. Don't just turn up for the party.

During the sixty, the press and scouts set up around me while I took my place near the starting line, an orange cone. Photographers fiddled with their cameras, selecting the right lenses. Scouts talked among themselves. Phones were whipped out. Other digital devices were set to record. I tuned out the chatter and locked in.

Breathe. Focus. It's game time.

A hush fell over the crowd. It was almost too quiet. I took a breath and exploded down the field toward a set of orange cones. Chest open and forward, I pumped my legs with every ounce of strength. Adrenaline shot through my body, numbing the pain of my torn oblique. I clocked in somewhere between a low of 6.6 and a high of 6.8 seconds. As I took a break to catch my breath and grab some water, scouts jotted down notes and press posted videos of the run on social media. After changing clothes and slapping on my glove, it was time to take some fly balls in the outfield. The next two-plus hours were much of the same. Drill, break. Drill, break. By the time I put on my batting gloves and started warming up in the cage, my oblique was on fire. During batting practice, when I squared off against the pitchers, I cleared a few fences and finished 8 for 19 in simulated game at bats.

When it was over, I had mixed feelings. I didn't think I did as well as I could have, but I definitely showed some potential. I could never prove the critics wrong or convince anyone that I could make my way to the majors. But that wasn't the point. I just wanted to demonstrate that this pursuit was serious. It wasn't a joke. It wasn't a publicity stunt. It wasn't a way to stay relevant. It was real.

Brodie and I sat down and talked to a few teams that afternoon, which was pretty awesome. I noticed there was one question that was asked the most: "Tim, you're used to being at the top of the professional sports chain; how do you feel about riding a bus?"

If you're not familiar with the structure of baseball, here are the basics. Most major league players are groomed in the minor league system. In some ways, the minors mirror the majors. In other ways, the two are miles apart. While the majors have only one level of talent and thirty teams from major cities, the minors have six tiers of talent and a total of 247 teams. In the farm system, you also play in front of a lot fewer people and make significantly less money than the big boys. Minor leaguers make an average of—wait for it— less than ten thousand dollars per year. Yeah, chump change. And while major leaguers travel on chartered planes and hole up in fancy hotels, minor leaguers ride a bus they hope will have air-conditioning and stay in whatever motel costs the least. No glamour here.

And that's where these scouts were going with the question of riding the bus. My response was quite simple: "If you don't know me, I get that question. But if you know anything about who I am, you'll know the answer. Listen, just a month ago I was in the Philippines riding the jeepney all over the country and taking bucket baths. I'm pretty sure I can handle for a short season in my life riding a Greyhound bus." (By the way, a jeepney is the standard mode of public transportation in the Philippines. This Philippine gas guzzler resembles a shorter version of a school bus and is painted in bold colors and adorned with religious symbols.)

Brodie told me later that all the teams who spoke with me left with an appreciation for my enthusiasm, talent, and hard work. This was good news. And now, I waited.

The buzz was out.

During the live workout, many had something to say. As always, there was promising feedback, as well as some nasty quips.

"The Tebow tryout is not controversial, or strange. It's great."

"He looked like an actor trying to portray a baseball player."

"Tim Tebow's workout was certainly good enough that someone will give him a chance."

"He looked quite awkward chasing balls in center field."

Someone said I was "fringe but serviceable." Another, "wildly strong but not in baseball shape."

After talking with the press, I headed back to Los Angeles. My body was running on little sleep, my oblique angry from the workout. I was wired. The adrenaline rush from this showcase was still kicking in high gear. I closed my eyes and prayed, *Well, I took the first step, God. I don't know what's going to happen next, but we're in this thing.*

While a number of teams gave me positive feedback, a total of five expressed interest in signing me. I spoke to the general managers of three teams and ultimately narrowed down the prospects to two—the Atlanta Braves and the New York Mets.

The Braves communicated well their belief in me but were nervous about all the hype that came along with me. Apparently, I come with a lot of public scrutiny.

I was excited to talk to Sandy Alderson, the general manager for the

Mets. I knew about his military background. I knew he was a pioneer of baseball's statistical world. I knew he was a great leader. These things made an impression on me before we even started talking.

Look, I knew I was an outlier and a long shot. Sandy saw me that way too. He knew I needed to be treated and trained like one. He did a great job communicating that he believed in me as a baseball player, that this wouldn't be a media circus, and, most importantly, that he was committed to creating a successful transition in the short term and for the long haul.

> I didn't know
> what to expect,
> but I was ready.
> Play ball.

I was really impressed when one of the first things he talked about on the phone was TTF. Sandy knew about the kids we help. He knew about the hospitals we build. This is a huge part of who I am as an individual, and he viewed this passion as something that could benefit the team as a whole. Sandy didn't just value bat speed or raw power; he also appreciated things like integrity, values, commitment, and leadership. Part of why he thought this could be a great partnership was because of what I could offer aside from baseball, intangibles like encouraging the younger guys and stepping up to be an example for others.

I felt a connection with Sandy. I thought he was authentic, and I appreciated his belief in me as a man, as an influencer, as a competitor, and as a potential ball player.

Know this was a tough decision. I prayed long and hard. I had conversations with Brodie and others, ad nauseam. Finally, because the talk with Sandy was convincing in so many ways, I chose to play with the New York Mets. And on September 8, 2016, I signed a minor league contract to play with that Big Apple team. (I'm back, New York!)

A little over a week later, I was sent to instructional league, then the

Arizona Fall League and spring training come February 2017. In April I started playing with the Mets affiliate the Columbia Fireflies. From the time I signed with the Mets, there was constant communication between the team and my agent about the developmental process. I was still on a learning curve when I played with Columbia in April and May. What was interesting was that my performance at home had always been better than my performance on the road. While trying to figure out why, by June I started to get on a roll and have better momentum. The Mets started judging me by my performance of late rather than the start of the season. By the end of June, I was promoted from low-A ball to St. Lucie of the high-A Florida State League. It was time to challenge myself on a higher level.

I didn't know what to expect, but I was ready. Play ball.

MAKE THIS YOUR DAY

All this talk about dreams may be bringing up some thoughts and feelings for you. Are you hearing any whispering in your heart? I believe God plants these aspirations in us for a reason. Particularly for us to take risks and act on them. Passion in this sense is more than just a superficial feeling. It's more than hype. It's more than motivation. It's more than excitement. It's deep, almost inexplicable. It might even be something that's engrained in our DNA. And it's something people can't take away.

You might have a passion to follow a dream, to start your own company, to rally a community together for a cause, to write a book. How do you know it's from God? How do you know it's not? How do you know it's something you should pursue or even spend time considering? These are tough questions to answer. I'm not in the business of telling people what to do, but I will say that it's important to have the courage to pursue what's in your heart if it lines up with what the Bible teaches. Pray about it. Seek wise counsel. Don't be afraid to take a risk. Don't let fear, criticism, or doubt cripple you from making a decision.

I shared a bit about the criticism that followed my pursuit of a baseball dream. Though the stakes were high and the naysayers loud, I didn't let that stop me from being committed to the journey.

**What are you willing to risk to follow a dream
or a passion in your heart?**

3

THIS IS THE DAY
Leave the Past Behind

Yesterday is gone. Tomorrow has not yet come. We have only today. Let us begin.

—Anonymous

've been sharing about my passion for baseball, how I trusted God with that desire and took a chance to chase that dream. You might be inspired right now to discern the desires of your own heart and think about the steps you need to take to pursue them. I want you to dream big!

Or, you might be rolling your eyes. Maybe you're thinking that because of the season of life you are in, you cannot afford the luxuries of the time or money it takes to go after something you really want. I get this.

Life looks different for everyone. We have different responsibilities, different challenges, and different schedules. And sometimes we have to do things in life that we don't necessarily want to do or that we don't have a passion for or that are just hard (like working two or three jobs to support a family). The idea alone of dreaming big or pursuing passion projects seems, well, extra. Whatever the case, it doesn't mean you have to waste your time doing things that are meaningless or carry little value.

Think about it this way. When you believe whose you are in Jesus and strive to thrive in your environment, you are in a way thanking Him for creating you, for being the perfect author of your faith and your life. What we think about God should reflect in what we do, how we live, and how we spend our time.

God created you with an awesome plan in mind. You were made for a purpose to do amazing things. I know so many people who can't wait to get the day over with so they can binge on whatever TV show is trending or numb their existence with other things. At the same time, most of these same people complain about how unfulfilled, bored, or tired they are.

Look, I know what it's like to want to get lost in an awesome movie or TV show. There's something to be said about enjoying artful entertainment. It can be powerful and can even inspire us. But often, this medium is used to escape reality. Whether intentional or not, it can be a means to neglect the truth of our lives. When we numb out on anything, we cannot see the joy, hope, and light that exist, even when life is hard. Nor can we imagine the incredible things God can do through us.

Some of our ability to thrive comes from our own perspective—how we view God, ourselves, and the world. Our view of God, for instance, changes how we view ourselves.

Think about how you view God for a moment. Do you believe your faith in God exists just to make you feel good? Do you think the miracle stories in the Bible—like the parting of the Red Sea, the resurrection of Lazarus, or the feeding of the five thousand—are simply stories frozen in time?

Or do you believe the same God who performed miracles thousands of years ago is the same yesterday, today, and forever? Do you believe that He can change your life? Do you believe that through you He can impact others in transformative ways? Do you believe God can change a life from darkness to light because you decide to step out in faith and give someone a message of hope?

Without having this mind-set, of course it's easy to numb out and watch Netflix for hours! Without a powerful view of God and knowing what's possible through Him, our capacity to thrive is completely diminished. When we begin to see God in a life-changing, miracle-making, and revolutionary way, we can have the courage to take a step of faith. We can do things outside our comfort zone. We can change our familiar routine and old patterns and do things differently, better.

Here's the challenge. What if we invested in things that had value? Like our relationship with God or our relationships with others. What if instead of complaining about what's not working in our lives, we tried to find a solution? What if we committed to improving our spiritual and physical health instead of feeling unfulfilled, sick, and tired all the time?

I find that the majority of people I come in contact with are problem finders. It's easy to point out problems. They're everywhere! But like I tell everyone who works with me and is part of our foundation, don't just tell me what's wrong with this or that; offer a solution. Don't be a problem finder. Be a problem solver.

> Don't be a problem finder. Be a problem solver.

I'm not saying I have the answers, but I do know that when we don't expect much from ourselves or especially from God, we stay stuck. We let life pass us by. We don't wake up and look at this day as an opportunity to live with purpose and passion. But, remember, this is what you were created for!

Maybe it's time to start praying and asking God to use whatever you have. Maybe it's time to pray that He would show you what you have. Whatever you've got, put it all in.

Is it time for you to start dreaming big, to start dreaming God-sized dreams? I don't know what that looks like for you. But I do know that part of living this way means being confident that regardless of what happens in life or with our pursuits, God's going to use it. He will use for the good our failures, our mistakes, our detours, and our U-turns, just like He will use our successes.

I'm always encouraged when I remind myself what Jesus said: "What is impossible for people is possible with God" (Luke 18:27). When I think about this in terms of baseball, I don't apply this truth to believe I'm going to one day be the best hitter in the majors. I believe it in the context of God doing more in my life, more with my dreams, more with my leap of faith, more with my love for Him and others than I could ever imagine.

MAGIC MOMENTS

It was my first appearance with the high-A St. Lucie Mets after being promoted from the Columbia Fireflies. We played a doubleheader that day, June 28, 2017. The sun beamed strong as clouds bobbed along the sky. Hot and humid, a typical Florida afternoon. My kind of day. I had gotten a single in the first game, but I knew I could do better.

Game two of the doubleheader. Bottom of the second. One of my former teammates from Columbia was on first base. I swung and missed on the first pitch slung by the Palm Beach Cardinals' Junior Fernandez. On the second, the umpire called out, "Ball!" He did the same for the third and fourth pitches. On the fifth pitch, Fernandez launched the ball at ninety-two miles per hour. I swung hard and met the pitch with a loud *crack*. The ball rocketed just left of the batter's eye screen in center field as fans erupted with a roar. I flew past first base and was headed toward second when I noticed my teammate freeze a few feet ahead of second base. He watched the ball sail over the fence; then he took off. In that fraction of a second, I knew I'd hit a home run.

I jogged toward home plate. I couldn't stop smiling. *Man, God, You helped me do it again!* It felt good making my way toward the dugout, swallowed by the sea of high fives and helmet taps. Though we lost the second game that day, I was proud to be able to contribute to my team.

The moment was similar to when I'd made my debut with the Fireflies on April 7, 2017. The loudspeakers blared my walk-up song, Jason Michael Carroll's "Where I'm From" as eighty-five hundred baseball fans cheered in the stands at Spirit Communications Park. With the temperature hovering in the low sixties and a stiff breeze blowing, it felt more like football weather. But there I was, gripping a baseball bat and heading toward home plate.

Augusta GreenJackets' left-handed pitcher Domenic Mazza, a 666th pick in the 2015 amateur draft and runner-up in golf's 2010 Re/Max World Long Drive Championship, warmed up on the mound.

It was the bottom of the second inning. Two outs and a man on third. Mazza lobbed the first pitch. I watched it whiz by. "Ball," the umpire yelled. I fouled off the next pitch, the ball flying behind the third-base dugout. On the third pitch, I swung. *Crack!* The ball flew high toward the left field center fence. The crowd exploded as I raced past first and toward second base. I thought I'd hit a double, so I hesitated until I heard the base umpire yell, "Keep going! Keep going!"

Adrenaline pumped through my body as I realized I had hit a home run on my first at bat in the minors. All I could think was, *Wow! That was a total God thing!* I felt pumped. *A home run on my first at bat.*

The same thing had happened when the Mets sent me down to instructional league in the fall of 2016. On September 28, I played my first organized baseball game since high school. On my first pitch in my first time up, I nailed a ninety-one-mile-per-hour pitch that flew over the center field fence in the Port St. Lucie ballpark. I had been aggressive, and what a great feeling seeing the support of my teammates, who mobbed me after I tapped home plate and started walking back to the dugout.

Whether it was a home run at the start of the journey, one right after being promoted, or others in between, here's the thing: In the bigger picture, it was just another game with plenty more to come. I would have opportunity after opportunity to wake up, work hard, and get better. This was all part of the process. The fact is, like all sports, baseball is filled with many highs and lows. So you can't make too much of any one thing.

My stats during instructional league and playing with the Scottsdale Scorpions in the Arizona Fall League during the fall of 2016 weren't as good as they could have been. While it motivated me to train more and work harder, I couldn't get discouraged. Again, I knew it was all part of the process. And I had a long way to go.

Every now and then, though, it's exciting to see the effort, the focus, and the hard work pay off—in my case at the time, in the form of home runs. I think God allows us to have great moments every now and then—like winning championships, making the sale of a lifetime, catching a break, getting an answer to prayer, experiencing a miracle. Our faith isn't dependent on miracles, but these moments help us stay the course and give us momentum to keep moving forward.

I know it's not crazy to hit a home run in a game, but it is pretty cool to do it on your first day in three different leagues. After each home run I hit, I would think, *Thanks, God. You let me do it again.* It wasn't that as a baseball player I was where I wanted to be at the time; rather, it was a reminder that He opened the doors for me to work hard and pursue this dream. God was in control of my life. He could take me from the bottom of the barrel to the top of the sky.

In my first year of minor league baseball, a lot of people made a big deal about all the fans who showed up. I was so grateful for the support, but I couldn't dwell on it. My priority was focusing on whatever was in front of me. So, whether I went 0 for 11 or was in the news for having contributed to the greatest rise in minor league baseball attendance in twenty-three years, I had only one job: Lock into this day. This game. This at bat.

THIS MOMENT, RIGHT NOW

When I announced my plans to pursue baseball, some worried that I would embarrass myself. My agents couldn't understand how I could possibly choose something that wasn't better for me financially or for my career or for my brand. But I believed in what I was doing. And that meant not only shutting down critics or people who couldn't understand this path but also refusing to let my present be defined by the past. This is something I had to do every single day.

I remember my first game during spring training for the Mets in March 2017. Spring training is an almost two-month series of practices and exhibition games right before the actual season starts. Eastern teams travel to Florida to play in the Grapefruit League, and western teams train in Arizona in the Cactus League. Everyone competes, from new prospects to seasoned veterans. It's a chance for the younger guys to try out for spots on the team and others to get their groove on for the coming season. I was invited to attend.

I'll never forget the game when I faced Red Sox right-hander Rick Porcello, the reigning American League Cy Young Award winner. Each year the Cy Young Award is given to the best pitcher in the major leagues, one each for the American League and National League. These pitchers are obviously no joke. And there I was, as green as could be, barely having warmed up before the game, facing the best pitcher in the league. Quite a matchup! In my first and only at bat against Porcello, I struck out.

A little over two weeks later, in another spring training game against the Washington Nationals, I faced Max Scherzer. He had already won the Cy Young Award, twice. Yeah, batting against Scherzer was a pretty big deal.

> Stop letting the past affect your present and your future.

Sporting a NY Mets jersey, number 97, I readied at the plate. Max hurled the first pitch, ninety-six miles per hour. I swung and missed. Strike one. Max fired again, ninety-seven miles per hour. Strike two. The third pitch clocked in at ninety-seven miles per hour. Strike three.

I found out a few days later that one of the players from the Nationals was taking five-hundred-dollar bets that I'd get a hit. I have a feeling this is why most of the pitches that were thrown that game fluctuated around the low nineties except when I was at bat.

The past is in the past. Like in football, I try not to allow the play before me to be affected by the play I just made. As an athlete, you can't let one day, one game, one play, a losing streak, or a string of home runs define anything. This is as true in life as it is in sports. I learned a long time ago to take things one day at a time. I have to focus on today and then when tomorrow comes, that day.

How about you? Are you not tapping into the potential of this day because of what happened yesterday or last year or ten years ago? Stop letting the past affect your present and your future.

I know. It's easier said than done, right? But it's possible.

The core of this problem is emotional attachment. If you are hanging on to negative emotions from an event, a mistake, or a failure in the past, you have no chance of competing or living at your highest level.

I'm a very emotional person, and I've had to learn over the years how important it is to control my emotions. Negative emotions will mess with you. They will keep you stuck. They will take you where you don't want to go. And they will keep you from being the person God has created you to be.

It's almost like you have to have a short-term memory. In terms of base-ball, if your last at bat wasn't great and you're up at the plate again, unless you're careful, fear, insecurity, and doubt will creep in. *Oh boy, what if I strike out again? That other player is doing so much better than me. I need to be more consistent like this guy.*

In order for the present play to be free of influence from the past, you have to lock in and focus. Some people will get in the box and concentrate on their breathing. Others will tune in to a slight change in their mechanics, whether that's shifting their weight or adjusting their grip.

In the movie *For Love of the Game*, Kevin Costner plays a veteran pitcher trying to prove himself. I love what he says when he's on the mound and try-ing to focus. He hears the sounds around him—the screaming fans, the vendors shouting up and down the stands, the commentary from the an-nouncer blaring through the speakers. It's loud. It's distracting. So he uses a trick for concentration; he says to himself, *Clear the mechanism.* In that mo-ment, he hears nothing. He locks into his catcher and the catcher's mitt. Fi-nally, he's ready to throw the pitch.

Do your best to clear your own mechanism. Stop. Breathe. Pray. Remind yourself that God doesn't judge you by your past. Nor should you. Remember what will help you right now. Questioning yourself will not have any benefit in the present. Nor will the crippling emotions of doubt, fear, or frustration.

Focus on what will make you better in this moment. Then take the next step. And the next. And the next. Do this and you start to change your mindset. You start to change your outlook. And through these day-by-day, step-by-step changes, you'll find you are starting to become your best you.

Learning Lessons

While the past does not define us, we can learn from it. We can use an experience when we did not perform at our best and do it better next time. I believe that though we are born with certain talents, traits, and tendencies, it doesn't mean we must be chained to them our whole lives. You may have always slept in late or snoozed a million times before actually getting up, but it doesn't mean you are destined to continue this behavior your whole life. You can discipline yourself to stop snoozing so often. You can choose to get to bed earlier. You can make little changes that over time will pay off in big ways.

I have a close friend who has been with me during some pretty stressful times. He asked me to coach him on something in particular. This friend has witnessed how my schedule often changes at the last minute, requiring a massive overhaul of my day or week. For example, when everything is planned to a T, from training to speaking, and suddenly four presidential candidates reach out at the same time and then I get a call from someone at the foundation who tells me one of our W15H kids just got put on hospice and wants to see me the same day I have an event that has been on my calendar for a year, things can get pretty hairy.

I find that most people either thrive in these spaces or get overwhelmed by them. Growing up with missionary parents, my siblings and I learned to acclimate to change and stress. I've watched my dad handle tough situations and seen our family rally under pressure. When bombs are going off in the village where you live and Dad takes off to see what's going on while Mom stays back to keep the five kids safe in the house, one learns quickly how to adapt. (You can read my second book, *Shaken,* for that story.) Participation in sports has also taught me a lot about how to thrive under pressure. When it's the fourth quarter and everyone's tired and muscles are aching, I want to be ready to go. In that moment, it's all about executing the two-minute drill.

My parents did a great job of making us kids strive to be successful in an uncomfortable environment. I can't tell you how many times they forced me to do things that didn't come naturally to me. For one, I wasn't comfortable speaking in public. Mom and Dad took notice of this early on and started signing me up to try out for plays. They made me pray out loud in front of others. They made me give presentations at science fairs. They registered me for local spelling bees.

I wasn't the greatest, or even good, at any of these things. Doing them was hard, and I hated it. With my dyslexia, reading and writing posed quite a challenge. I could barely spell the word *cat,* and there I was on a stage in front of one hundred people trying to spell *procrastinate.* But here's the thing: The more uncomfortable situations I found myself in over the years, the better I got at handling them. I've had to learn and work and improve and grow. I may not be the best at certain things, but I know how to rise to the occasion and do my best.

It's easy in stressful situations to see the "can'ts" or the "won'ts" that get in our way. Instead, we have to see the positives, what we can do, fix, or change in that moment. One of the greatest temptations is to worry instead of pray, trust God, and take action. Worry won't change anything. When you're able to shift your perspective to see what's possible, you have a greater chance of having a positive outcome.

Tackling stress instead of cracking under pressure may not come easy for you, but with time, practice, and effort, anyone can learn to be clutch. Remember the friend I talked about at the beginning of this section? The one who asked me to coach him? Together we worked on creating strategies to handle moments when the stakes are high, like how to break down a situation, clear out what doesn't need to be there, create a solution to the problem, and finally settle on a decision. I'll say that he's gotten so much better at this. It may be hard to learn a crucial skill or unlearn a character trait that is not working for you, but with time and effort, you'll get there.

DON'T LOOK BACK

When I was playing for the Columbia Fireflies, a reporter asked me, "Has there been any moment where you said, 'Man, I should have stuck with baseball [when I was young]?'" This question got me fired up. I told him,

> I think in life there are times when negativity and doubt and fear creep in. We have a choice in those moments. What are we going to do with those thoughts? How are we going to handle them? And what's the next step? Having these thoughts isn't a bad thing; it's what you do with them.
>
> For me it's about, first, going back to the truth that everything happens for a reason and, second, trusting in God's plan. I took this crazy route filled with highs and lows for a reason, and at the same time I'm doing something I love. So I'm not going to look back with regret. I could look back on my time with football and say, "Right

now I could be beating this guy or that team," but there's no point. Instead I say, "God, I trust You. I thank You for the opportunity to play ball. And I'm going to go balls out every chance I have to play."

My journey in football, my road in baseball—they're both part of my story. God didn't make mistakes when I was going through the highs or the lows, nor with how my path in professional sports turned out. He wrote my story before I was even born. With this truth in mind, I don't have to look back. My job is to stay in the moment and do the best I can at whatever is before me.

While there are always things I could look back on and wish I did better or could change, I don't want to live in the past. When you keep wondering what could have been or what you should have done differently, here's what happens: you miss the present moment and cripple your potential in the future.

> Life is not about surviving. It's about thriving.

Sure, I could have asked God over and over why my football career ended before I thought it would or why I didn't stick with baseball in the first place, but when you start asking "why" in excess, what you're really saying is, "God, I don't trust You." Just because life doesn't go our way or the dreams we have don't come true according to our wishes, it doesn't change the meaning and purpose of our lives.

I don't know how this part of my story will end. One thing is certain: I'm going to keep stepping off the edge of the cliff and trusting God.

I think about my parents. When they left the comforts of home in the United States to move to the Philippines with four kids and start a ministry on the other side of the world, they didn't look back. They trusted God with the plan for their lives. My mom recently told me how there were multiple times when they had less than a hundred dollars in their bank account and barely enough food to feed our family. Mom would ask Dad, "What now? What do we do?" Dad didn't let fear get ahold of him. He took risks, God-sized risks. His answer was always the same. He would tell her, "We give the money away, Pam." Crazy, right? Doesn't make sense. But whenever Dad stepped off the edge of this cliff and trusted God, God would provide. Every time they would give their last penny away, in nothing short of a miracle, someone would stop by and give my parents either food or money. Every single time.

I've discovered in my life that the more I'm able to step off the edge of a cliff and take a risk, the more I'm fulfilled. I believe this is true for everyone. The more we clear out of our comfort zones, the more opportunity we have to experience God's faithfulness. The more we trust Him instead of what others say, the more our faith grows. The more we choose to seek after the desires we believe God has put on our hearts, the more we really live.

Life is not about surviving. It's about thriving. When someone in that room two-plus years ago said pursuing baseball would ruin my brand, I disagreed. My life is bigger than my brand.

I'm not trying to build a brand; I'm living a life. My life.

MAKE THIS YOUR DAY

Most of us have failed at something, whether a business idea that ultimately flopped, plans we carefully calculated, or a relationship we didn't handle well. If you're ambitious, want to try new things, or live life differently, guess what? You're going to fail. You're going to make a mistake (or two). You're going to mess up.

This reminds me of a quote I've often heard: "Never let success get to your head. Never let failure get into your heart."

Here's some good news: if you've messed up, that's not the worst thing that can happen. What's worse is not trying, sitting out of the game instead of taking the shot. The only way to get unstuck is to keep trying and, more importantly, give it everything you've got.

I've known many quarterbacks, pitchers, and other great athletes who stopped performing at their best because of a failure or a mistake they made. They didn't lose their potential to be great; they just were more focused on what had happened in the past.

You might be in that same place. If so, I want to challenge you to move forward. While you can't change the fact that you failed, here's what you *can* do. Admit that it happened. Then learn from it. Finally, be ready in the now. Don't waste time and energy worrying that you'll repeat the same mistake. Lock in. Concentrate on where you are in this moment. And make it your best.

The past doesn't have to define you, but you can use it to motivate what you do in this moment, in this day.

What can you do today to refuse to allow the past to cripple your present?

4

Listen to the Right Voice

I am not who others say I am. I am who
God says I am.

The bus bumped along a stretch of unfamiliar highway. Some of my team-mates dozed off on stiff seats, while others tried to catch some sleep on air mattresses squeezed in the narrow aisle. I was watching a movie on my iPad, but fading. Though my body was tired, I felt more emotionally drained than anything. The last few games at the end of May 2017—two months into my first minor league season—had been rough. And I had no idea how much time was left in the eight-plus-hour drive back home from Kentucky.

The Fireflies had spent the last two weeks climbing up the East Coast to New Jersey, then back home to Columbia, South Carolina, where we played the West Virginia Power and the Charleston RiverDogs. After getting rained out in one game against the RiverDogs and taking a loss in another, we got back on the road again and headed to Lexington, Kentucky, to contend with the Legends.

Our series against the Legends had not been my best. The team had won two out of four games, but I wasn't thrilled with my performance. My first at bat in game one was a walk. My second, I grounded out. Then I struck out my third and fourth at bats. I vowed to do better the next game, except I didn't play that day. In our third game, I popped out once and struck out twice. The final game of the series didn't end well. I struck out my first at bat. Then my second. And then the third. I was 0 for 9 that series. Talk about a slump.

Funny, during those games the Legends' production staff took the opportunity to poke some fun at me. By now I've realized that people are going to say good things about me and bad things about me. And none of these things get to define who I am. In the Legends' ballpark, there were two large video screens in the outfield. Pregame and between plays during the game, images of me were blasted on the screen. One such picture was of me running in the rain without a shirt on during football practice when I was with the Jets. Then, whenever I was at bat, the monitors blared a picture of the Kentucky Wildcats football player who in a college game nine years earlier had sacked and knocked me unconscious. Sometimes they'd run clips of me throwing interceptions. I tried not to pay much attention.

During the season this kind of thing happened often when I was on the road. In another away game, one of the announcers held a contest on the field where one fan would throw a football to another fan. When the ball was caught, the announcer would say something like, "Well, looks like you're the best quarterback in the park!"

About a month later, when the Fireflies were playing against the River-Dogs, the same kind of thing happened but with even more theatrics. The team's mascot, a man in a dog costume they call Charlie T., ran around the stadium wearing eye black with John 3:16 written on it and, of course, he Tebowed on the field.

When I was at bat, the "Hallelujah Chorus" would blast throughout the ballpark. And whenever a fellow teammate was at the plate, scribbled above his picture posted on the scoreboard were the words "Not Tim Tebow," and in the background flashed a picture of me crying after the Gators lost to the Crimson Tide in the 2009 SEC championship game. I'm pretty sure the RiverDogs' powers that be apologized publicly at some point.

There were times that first season, particularly if I was in a slump, when I wondered what I was doing there. I'd be tempted to listen to the voices of insults or even the ones of doubt in my own head. I never wanted to give up on this dream—it wasn't an option. I didn't mind the grind of baseball, and I'm accustomed to being poked fun at. But when you're not doing as well as you want, if you're not careful, you can start tuning in to the whispers of doubt.

> I never wanted to give up on this dream— it wasn't an option.

I remember being on the road with the Fireflies in April and playing in North Carolina the same day as the NFL draft. Some of the picks were announced and shown on the screen. It was a weird feeling. I was flooded with memories of getting drafted myself. I didn't regret my decision to pursue baseball, nor did I get stuck on memory lane thinking about football. It just felt . . . weird.

Often, I'd think about Dad and wonder if I should be with him instead of on the road. I wrestled with what was more important. But knowing how much Dad believed in me and in what I was doing, I would remind myself of what he would say: "Stay right where you are, son. Keep doing what you're doing."

Different thoughts like these would pop into my head, especially on our long road trips.

Oh, speaking of the bus, if you're curious what it was like riding the bus, it was like, well, riding a bus for two or eleven hours. Sometimes I'd try to get lost in a good movie. Sometimes I'd head to the back of the bus and play Mafia with the guys. Sometimes I'd talk to or FaceTime with friends and family and feel more connected to home. There were times I felt lonely, as being the oldest player on the team put me in a different stage of life than my teammates.

Whether I was on the bus or playing on our home field, I had to be careful with what I allowed to consume my mind and turn off the voices that would try to bring me down.

TURN UP THE VOLUME

The fact is, when you face challenges of any kind, you're going to hear voices. It doesn't matter how much success you've had or how much you've overcome in the past. When you decide to do something different or pursue something bigger, voices will creep in.

The Enemy will whisper lies in your ear. He'll tell you, *You've tried your best. This is obviously not working out well. Just call it a day.* Sometimes critics will tell you to stop reaching for something because it's too hard, you're not qualified, or it's a waste of time. Many times, the voices of discouragement we hear come from our own mouths or thoughts.

I heard in my heart things like, *You've already accomplished a lot. Why risk so much for baseball? Just be comfortable. Take a cozy gig.* Sometimes I'd hear the voices of others, like some in the baseball community who hated what I was doing because they believed I made their profession a joke.

So what do you do when these voices start to overwhelm you to the point that you can't hear much else? Believe that God has a plan and a purpose for your life. Believe that He is in control of your life. Believe that whatever happens, however and wherever the road you're walking on unwinds, He's got this (see Ephesians 2:10; Psalm 119:114).

Let me make this more practical. Here are two ways to do this: One, speak into your own life. And two, turn up the voice that matters.

Whenever I struggled at the plate, I chose to remember that this desire to play baseball was with me since I was a little boy. I chose to believe that God planted this dream inside my heart even before I was born. And while I don't always do this audibly, I would vocalize my faith. I would speak truth into my life. One of my heroes in the Bible, King David, did this (see 1 Samuel 30:6). It might seem silly, but it's actually very encouraging.

Sometimes, you need to do this out loud. It's amazing what an incredible difference hearing yourself speak words of encouragement will have on your mind-set, your outlook on life, and the moments that may get you down. If you don't block out the negativity, the loneliness, or the questions, they will fester and take hold of you.

Feeling bombarded by doubt, fear, or skepticism isn't bad in and of itself. It comes down to how you are going to handle it. I mentioned this in the last chapter. I remember in some games seeing teammates, after not getting the hits they wanted, leave the batter's box furious. Been there, done that. It was interesting to me, though, how many of these guys as they were walking away from the plate slammed their helmets on the ground or threw their bats in a rage. I'll admit, when I was disappointed after striking out three times in a row, there were times I would have liked to chuck my bat into right field and let out some steam. But, really, what would have been the point? It's not like throwing something in anger is going to have any positive effect and make me crush my next at bat. Speaking into my life, however, will have a positive effect.

When things were not going my way in baseball, I had a choice. I could sulk and pout, or I could lock into something positive. So I did what I had to do. I motivated myself. I hyped myself up. I'd say in my mind something like, "I believe during my next at bat, I will get on a winning streak."

This takes work and focus. And time. Do yourself a favor. Try it. Speak into your life. And keep speaking into your life. Then see what happens. Though things might still not turn in your favor on the outside, you'll sense a shift in your spirit. And with more time, you'll begin to encourage yourself naturally instead of forcing it.

Doing great things, things that matter, things that make a difference, will open the door to doubt, to fear, and to criticism from others. But we control the volume in whatever voices clamor for our attention. We don't have to give in to or believe everything we hear.

Ask yourself, "What voices am I turning up?" The voices of self-doubt? The voices of your enemies? The voices of insecurity? Or are you turning up the volume of the One who has a plan for your life, the One who in all things brings purpose and meaning, the One who has you where you are for a reason? Choose to listen to that voice!

One of the most amazing truths in the Bible is that through faith in Jesus I have been adopted by God. When I feel closest to God is when I think of Him as my heavenly Father. Not just Lord of all or Creator of the universe or the Maker of Adam or Eve or someone to call on for help, but Dad. I consider myself fortunate for having the greatest father on earth, but I know not everyone can say the same thing. You may have had a terrible dad who may have even abandoned or abused you in some way. I am so sorry if you had that experience.

Whatever your dad was like growing up, try to picture with me what a great father does. He forgives you—always. He listens when you talk. And he talks even when you don't want him to. He disciplines you when you need it, but it hurts him to. He stands in the way of danger and shields you. He takes punishment meant for you but never says it's your fault. He stares danger in the face, puts his life on the line, and even offers to die in your place.

My earthly dad is amazing, but my heavenly Father is my best friend. Through our faith in Jesus, we are adopted into God's family and become children of the king of the world who will forever reign.

When the voices of doubt, confusion, or hurt get so loud you don't know what to do, remember to listen to the voice of the One who will always love you and will never let you down.

WHAT GOD SAYS IS MOST IMPORTANT

Many times, our opinion of God is affected by what other people have said to us, more than likely the same people that we probably shouldn't have listened to in the first place.

I know what it feels like to be deeply disappointed by something someone said. Over the years, I've talked with different coaches and have been in meetings with different general managers who've assured me, in their own words, "Tim, I've got your back. And I'm going to fight for you." But when it was crunch time, their words were meaningless. They didn't have my back. And they certainly didn't fight for me.

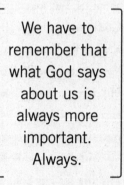

We have to remember that what God says about us is always more important. Always.

You may have had a similar experience of someone saying one thing and doing another. This can be discouraging. It's just as hurtful as when someone says something negative right to your face. This reminds me of when I attended an Atlanta Thrashers hockey game after winning the

Heisman Trophy. I was enjoying the game and the company of some of my siblings, when all of a sudden I looked up and realized I was on the jumbotron. The crowd went nuts. And not in a good way. Thousands of fans erupted in that stadium, pointing at me on the screen and chanting—in unison—a very colorful (and not in a good way) four-letter word with my name. The place became a madhouse. So much chaos ensued around us, in fact, that security swooped down near our seats and ushered us to a different section. From an outside perspective, one could say that everyone in that space hated me. What's funny, though, is that after the game, I was bombarded with requests for selfies and autographs. What's up with that?

Whether people are negative to us directly or behind our backs, in words or actions, we have to remember that what God says about us is always more important. Always. What He says matters more than criticism, more than lies, more than the taunts of a bully, more than false accusations, more than any hate-filled words hurled at us.

It may be difficult to trust God after being broken, rejected, betrayed, or gossiped about. The negative voices of the past can overpower what God says about us. But we cannot let what others have said or done taint His truth. God is trustworthy. The psalmist wrote, "O my people, trust in him [God] at all times. Pour out your heart to him, for God is our refuge" (Psalm 62:8). We can read the Bible and trust God's promises. We can trust His plan and His purpose for our lives. It's important to be encouraged by others and even encourage ourselves, but the most uplifting and life-changing encouragement we will ever get comes from God alone.

Three times while Jesus was on earth, God spoke out of heaven affirming His love for His Son, Jesus, and endorsing Him on His mission. Jesus was able to endure tremendous suffering for the sake of others because He listened to the voice of His Father. Today, God's voice can give you the confidence you need to endure life's challenges.

MAKE THIS YOUR DAY

When you choose to live based on what God says and not what others say, you can live with confidence. You can live secure. You can live knowing He loves you, He cares for you, He has a plan for you, and He has a purpose for your life.

You can trust God's voice!

Here are some Bible verses that have helped remind me of what God says about me. I pray they encourage you as well.

- God made me wonderfully complex and marvelous. (See Psalm 139:14.)
- I am a child of God. (See Galatians 3:26.)
- I am God's masterpiece. (See Ephesians 2:10.)
- God's hand is always on me. (See Psalm 139:5.)
- As a child of God, I am a special treasure. (See Exodus 19:5.)
- God loves me with an unfailing love. (See Jeremiah 31:3.)
- I am chosen by God. (See 1 Thessalonians 1:4.)

If you're feeling discouraged by the voices of doubt or other negative voices, how can God's Word encourage you?

5

Believe in What Really Matters

The goal is not to be rich, famous, or powerful. The goal is to impact as many people as possible for something good, for something right.

'll never forget when one of the girls I had dated finally hit a certain number of followers on social media. I'd never before seen her get so excited. I was happy for her, of course, but it made me wonder why it meant so much.

Being popular mattered. I can't say it mattered the most to her, but it was pretty high on her list. It seemed she sought after the false security of being famous instead of the satisfaction she could get from trying to impact others for the better. It made me sad because I knew what a great and big heart she had. I saw the best in her. I wished she could see what I could see.

It's amazing how when we're feeling society's pressures or going through a difficult season, our focus tends to be self-centered. We get so fixed on what others tell us is important or what we're feeling or what we don't have that we get stuck. It's easy to lose perspective.

I was thinking recently about our annual TTF Celebrity Gala and Golf

Classic. This is our foundation's biggest fund-raiser of the year. Everyone gets dressed up real fancy for the gala. I'm talking black tie for some. We host these parties so that we can make a difference in the lives of others. We wear our suits and fancy dresses on the outside so that people who have been forgotten, who may never have a chance, or who don't know that God loves them can understand what real worth is on the inside.

Before each gala, some of my friends and I take bets of who among us is going to be the best dressed. And that night we bring out the big guns, fashion-wise. None of us wins, of course. All we do is argue and vote for ourselves. Side note: I'd like to think I deserve the title each time. But, hey, this is not about me.

After our gala in 2017, I remember being convicted of this. Now, there's nothing wrong with getting dressed up and wanting to look nice. I haven't always been super into fashion, but I've gotten more into it as of late. It's about perspective. There are times we can get so caught up with being the coolest, the best dressed, the one with the most Instagram followers, or the most popular that we forget the people in this world who may not be what society considers cool, who can't even afford a dress or a suit, or who have few, if any, Instagram followers.

Having the right perspective of what we ought to value reminds me of a passage in the Bible. In Luke 14, Jesus, as He often did, makes a social distinction contrary to popular opinion. He is having dinner in the home of a Pharisee, one of the religious leaders in the community. Noticing His fellow dinner companions were rushing to seat themselves at the head of the table, Jesus offers a suggestion:

When you are invited to a wedding feast, don't sit in the seat of honor. What if someone who is more distinguished than you has also been invited? The host will come and say, "Give this person your seat." Then you will be embarrassed, and you will have to take whatever seat is left at the foot of the table!

Instead, take the lowest place at the foot of the table. Then when your host sees you, he will come and say, "Friend, we have a better place for you!" Then you will be honored in front of all the other guests. For those who exalt themselves will be humbled, and those who humble themselves will be exalted. (verses 8–11)

Then Jesus turns to the host and gives him an even more counterculture message:

When you put on a luncheon or a banquet . . . don't invite your friends, brothers, relatives, and rich neighbors. For they will invite you back, and that will be your only reward. Instead, invite the poor, the crippled, the lame, and the blind. Then at the resurrection of the righteous, God will reward you for inviting those who could not repay you. (verses 12–14)

So many times, we as Americans look on the outside for what we value. God, however, looks on the inside.

Perspective.

A BETTER PERSPECTIVE

It can be easy to get caught up in what society or social media tells us is important. Thankfully, God's perspective is very different. His perspective always reaches outward and is viewed with an eternal light. When we strive to view life this way, we can begin to see a bigger picture at work. And we can begin to understand what's most important.

When I think about the baseball games that were special, they weren't just the ones where I hit a home run or improved my stats. I was touched by the thousands of people who came to support me throughout the season, not because I was a great athlete, but because of things I had done outside football or baseball.

I remember one road trip where I was welcomed by a crowd of fifty or sixty people wearing Night to Shine T-shirts. These were volunteers who gave their time, resources, and hearts to people some would think less of. During the entire season, I saw thousands of supporters—many who had special needs and their families. I can't tell you how many people showed up to each game. I would spend time with them, and they would tell me their stories, sharing how hard the journey was and how God was helping them through it—man, these people helped me keep the right perspective. And it was so uplifting to meet people who got help from our foundation or were encouraged by a talk I gave somewhere. It was a reminder that my life is bigger than my batting average, more than throwing or catching a ball.

I never want to get so caught up in sports that I start to define myself by what happens in those three hours of a game. I think about my senior year in college. The pressure was on, so much at times that it felt crushing. I became consumed with trying to win three out of four championships and getting another Heisman. Life became more than a game, but in a different way. In my senior year, the Gators were undefeated, 12–0. We were number one in the country, on top of the world. What a feeling!

And then, on December 5, 2009, we lost the SEC championship to Alabama. I cried. Literally. It felt like everything came crashing down. Our team still made an impact in the world of college football. We even finished third in the country. It was a good season by some standards; some would even say a great season, but not by our standards.

During that time, it was hard for me to keep everything in perspective. It was all about the game, all about the legacy, all about Florida, all about making a mark. Don't get me wrong, these are all good reasons to want to crush it. But it wasn't everything. And it wasn't what mattered most.

———

In my first year in professional baseball, it was so much easier to have the right perspective. This didn't mean I wanted to go 0 for 9 or that I didn't want to smash a ball out of the park. It just meant that the game wasn't everything.

More than getting to the majors, I want to be a believer. A believer, first and foremost, in God. I want to also be a believer in my teammates, a believer in my abilities, a believer in why I'm here. I want to be a believer in people too. I want to bring the best out in others, from those who are closest to me to those I meet for the first time. I want people's lives to be better because they know me.

> More than getting to the majors, I want to be a believer. A believer, first and foremost, in God.

You know what's awesome? In everything we do, we have a chance to influence. In fact, one of the greatest things we can do in life is influence other people for the better.

I believe that every time we meet someone, it never ends in neutral. Their experience of us is either positive or negative. Think about the people you encounter in your own life. Ever notice how some are life givers and others are life takers? Sure, there is an exception to every rule. But I've found most people fall into one of those two categories. The big idea here is that every opportunity you have with someone is an opportunity to influence that person for the good.

One of my favorite things to do in sports is to rally my teammates to believe that together we can accomplish something special. Recently, one of our foundation's W15H kids reminded me of something that happened in a Broncos versus Bears game in 2011.

With less than three minutes remaining on the clock, we were down 10–0. I scrambled to the right and hit Demaryius Thomas for a ten-yard touchdown, which set us up for a dramatic overtime victory. We took it home with a field goal, 13–10. Another fourth-quarter comeback!

Earlier, Demaryius, an amazing receiver whom I trusted, missed an important play. I could tell he was disappointed. I know the feeling. Nobody wants to let his team down. At one point after that play, I approached Demaryius and said, "Buddy, you've got this. You're good. And I believe you're going to have the chance to catch the game winner." Now, I didn't know for sure that would happen. But I believed it. And I wanted Demaryius to believe it too. Sure enough, though not the game winner, he caught the touchdown pass that gave us the opportunity to win the game.

When I was young, I would watch college football every Saturday. At halftime of each game, my brothers and I would jump off the couch and run outside to play an impromptu game of football. We rotated between three positions: quarterback, defensive back, and wide receiver. Whatever position we played, we pretended we were a college (or NFL) player we admired or had just got done watching and tried to play like that person. For example, I'd pretend to be Charles Woodson intercepting passes and running them all the way back. Sometimes I'd pretend to be Jerry Rice on a slant, running a beautiful, crisp route. Other times I was Steve Young on an amazing scramble.

Whether we realize it or not, people are watching us. What we say and what we do matter. When we live with purpose, we can make a difference that can leave a lasting impact. So whether you're sailing in the highs of life or just trying to survive the lows, remember that your life matters. And what you do for others matters.

TRANSCEND THE JOURNEY

In everything I've done in my sports journey, I've tried to make it bigger than just the action of the game. I've turned successes and failures into teachable moments, stories I've used to encourage others. That's the special thing about sports. There are opportunities to see beyond what God is doing in your life in the present moment. This happens when you serve the One who always has a greater purpose in mind in whatever you do.

During my first baseball season while playing with the Port St. Lucie Mets, on one of our road trips, I was working out at a local gym with some of my teammates. My routine kept getting interrupted by random people wanting to say hello. I was happy to stop what I was doing to chat with these sweet folks, but by the fourth or fifth interruption and having to restart unfinished sets multiple times, my patience was running thin. Frustrated, I left with two of my teammates. We headed across the street to Publix, a local grocery store. *Might as well pick up some snacks for the road.*

I was over by the meat section when I noticed a woman walking with a boy I believed was her son. He looked eighteen or nineteen and evidenced mannerisms that indicated he might be autistic. The young man walked with his eyes glued to the floor, constantly fiddling with his hands.

I walked by them a few times on purpose. Maybe they would recognize me from my foundation's work with people who have special needs. They didn't. The mom was preoccupied trying to keep her son close while checking off items on her shopping list.

I grabbed some protein drinks and a bag of almonds and headed toward the checkout lane. As I got closer to the front of the store, I saw this woman and her son in line to pay. I stepped up right behind them, as did a trail of people who had been following me throughout the store. As this one asked for an autograph and that one asked for a picture, I noticed from the corner of my eye the woman with her son looking over at me. When the commotion finally died down, she tapped me on the arm and said, "Excuse me. What's your name?"

"Tim," I replied, smiling.

She thought for a moment. "And what's your last name?"

"Tebow. My name is Tim Tebow."

Then it clicked. She grabbed me and started crying. Falling tears led to loud sobs as she buried her face in my arm. Finally, trying to catch her breath, she grabbed her son and said, "That prom that you went to? The one where you got all dressed up? This is the man who put it on for you."

Her son, who hadn't even given me eye contact until that point, looked straight at me. A big smile stretched over his face. Then he, too, started crying.

The coolest part of meeting these two amazing people was that this woman had no idea I was an athlete. Her son didn't have a clue either. The only reason they knew me was because I loved that young man enough to help sponsor a prom for him. (I'm talking about my favorite night of the year, our foundation's Night to Shine. This movement celebrates people who have special needs. TTF hosts proms all over the world where we crown each guest as prom king or queen.)

We talked for a few minutes before parting ways. This woman told me her son attended Night to Shine the first two years of its inception. He couldn't attend the third because of medical complications. She told me how hard it was to parent a child with special needs, saying how something as simple as going to the grocery store created much anxiety for her. Whenever she had to run an errand or go somewhere, this woman never knew whether her son was going to have an outburst that would require them to leave immediately or whether it was going to be a relatively smooth process.

> God can do
> something
> significant
> in whatever
> your hands
> find to do.

I listened, nodding. I can't even imagine what this woman and other parents who have children with special needs go through each day. "Well," I said, "hopefully we'll have a prom for your son every year. And I have a feeling he'll make the next one."

In this powerful moment, I felt God reminding me in my heart that there's a reason for everything. There was a reason I cut my workout short. There was a reason I went to Publix. And even in my frustration at the gym, which happened to fall in the morning, this was the day that had purpose. This moment was so powerful, in fact, it prompted me to start thinking of writing this book. I left Publix that morning a different person than when I walked in.

Although pursuing my dream and giving it everything I've got is important, life is more than just crushing every game. It's about meaning and purpose. It's about believing in whatever you do, whether you're a stay-at-home parent changing diapers and feeding babies, an executive running meetings and making sales, or a college student turning in papers and studying for exams. God can do something significant in whatever your hands find to do.

This is the day to let God do just that, even when you least expect it.

Believe, No Matter the Circumstances

Life is challenging. None of us are immune to tough times, to seasons of doubt, to trials that seem like they'll never end, to obstacles that seem impossible to overcome. But even in trying spaces, we can still choose to believe that God will use these hardships for good. We can choose to believe that He can change us in the midst of them. We can choose to believe that when we turn to Him, God can turn even our darkest days into light.

After making my debut in the Arizona Fall League in October 2016, I spent time with some fans who waited for me after the game. Most of my teammates had gone into the locker room while I signed autographs by the third-base line. I remember scribbling my name on a baseball when suddenly, gasps broke out.

As I turned my head to the left, my eyes fell on a twentysomething man wearing a baseball cap and sunglasses. I remembered seeing him behind some people I had signed something for just a minute earlier. It happened so fast, but I recall watching in shock as he convulsed and then fell to the ground, seemingly unconscious.

I rushed over and yelled for someone to get help. I'm not a paramedic, so I had no idea whether this man was unconscious or, God forbid, dead. I did the only thing I knew to do in that moment: pray. I quietly reached over the barrier in front of the first row, and with my hand on his leg, I prayed under my breath for this man in need. I'll never forget right after saying "God, please heal him," this young man's eyes burst wide open and he gasped violently.

As he slowly came to while medical personnel were on their way, I started talking to him. He told me his name was Brandon. He had epilepsy and had just had a seizure. Somewhere in the beginning of our ten- or fifteen-minute conversation, Brandon admitted to being a Georgia Bulldogs fan. Game on! I had no choice but to give him a hard time about it.

"Maybe I should have prayed for you in a different way," I said, laughing, "or prayed for your emotional healing."

Noticing Brandon's Batman T-shirt, we started debating superheroes. Who was better, Batman or Superman? He made a good case for Batman. But to me, there was no contest. Nobody beats Superman.

Brandon and I stayed in touch afterward. Hearing his story in the series of conversations we've had since meeting has been inspiring. On May 28, 2013, Brandon was diagnosed with epilepsy. While no one knows for sure, one of his doctors thinks the condition resulted from a brain injury when he dove into a pool at the age of seventeen. Since his diagnosis, Brandon's had at least 250 seizures. Because of the epilepsy, he can't work much, he can't drive, and he has serious dietary restrictions.

Brandon told me, "For the past few years I was mad at God. I was angry about having epilepsy. I was angry about not being able to enjoy a full life." But something happened the morning of the game. Brandon saw his doctor for a regular checkup. When he walked out the front door of the office, he felt in the pit of his stomach that things needed to change. He didn't like the person he was becoming. The anger was consuming. A Christian, he also felt far from God. While the distance made him feel empty, he knew he was the one who had pushed God away.

Brandon knew his life could be different, better. Focusing on not having the kind of life he thought he deserved wasn't working anymore. So that afternoon, this young man decided to do something that he loved—watch a baseball game. It would turn out to be more than a sporting event. It would be life changing. In his words,

I sat down before the game started and felt God nudging at my heart. I couldn't help but overhear a conversation happening behind me. A reporter from the *New York Times* and a spectator were talking about God. I felt a tug in my heart to talk to the one man. So after the reporter had left, I introduced myself. We started chatting about faith. I told him I had epilepsy. He told me his son had it too. We talked more and I shared how far I felt from God. In that moment, this stranger prayed for me, and I rededicated my life to Jesus. I felt free. I felt changed. I felt reborn. Three hours later, after the game ended, I headed down to the third-base line to see if I could get an autograph from Tim. But as I walked down the steps, I started to get a metal taste in my mouth. I knew a seizure was coming. Next thing I knew, I was waking up on the concrete floor. I was disoriented, hallucinating that Tim Tebow was standing over me and praying for me.

Of course, it was no hallucination.

The next day, I talked to Brandon. Doctors were certain the seizure was caused by the heat. Then, great news. This young man experienced a miracle. While over the years Brandon has undergone countless EEGs, a test to diagnose epilepsy and monitor brain activity, doctors were never able to perform one during or immediately after a seizure. This was important, because the test could help doctors figure out the severity of the disease and the right treatment plan. When Brandon underwent an EEG after his seizure at the ballpark, doctors were able for the first time to pinpoint the seizure activity and ultimately determine the right dosage and type of medication he needed. This was, indeed, a miracle.

While Brandon may need to be on medication for the rest of his life, since renewing his faith, his life has changed. He's back in church. He's learning more about the Bible. He is starting to share his story with others. Each week he takes a train into downtown Phoenix to encourage the homeless. On our foundation's service day, Brandon organized a water drive with local food pantries. And on the anniversary of recommitting his faith in Jesus the day we met, Brandon started an annual tradition of doing something nice for someone, all day long. This past year, he bought coffee for over twenty people.

> "We get knocked down, but we are not destroyed."

Brandon is a light to many. He loves to quote 2 Corinthians 4:8–9: "We are pressed on every side by troubles, but we are not crushed. We are perplexed, but not driven to despair. We are hunted down, but never abandoned by God. We get knocked down, but we are not destroyed." Brandon still has tough days, but he knows God is with him every step of the way.

I'm so proud of Brandon. He is an inspiration for many reasons. One of them is that in the midst of his physical and health challenges, he was able to focus on what really matters, his relationship with God. Brandon's attitude is incredible. He could have continued to dwell on his epilepsy and the difficulties it presented in his life. Instead, he is focusing on what he can do for God. He is using his trials as a testimony. He is allowing God to use him in any way. This is powerful stuff!

Do you think before he was given the assignment, Noah ever thought to himself, *One day I'm going to build an ark and save a bunch of people from destruction by a flood*? Do you think Moses woke up one day and believed he was going to be part of the reason the people of Israel would be free from Egypt? Do you believe that as a boy David knew he was going to someday crush a giant with a stone? I doubt it. I'm sure it was hard for these guys to see the vision. But when they were called by God, they stepped out in faith. And despite their insecurities, they believed more in what God could do through them than in what they were capable of on their own.

MAKE THIS YOUR DAY

Are you risking enough in your spiritual life that you put what you have on the line so God can show up in a big way? I know it can be hard to do, but it's always worth the reward. Often, we live so cautiously that we never give God a chance to come through. You don't have to have a dream to play ball or rule the world. Risk what you have for the sake of helping other people and seeing what God can do in your life and in the lives of others. Put yourself out there and do something that might terrify you or make you uncomfortable, like sharing your testimony for the first time or telling a stranger God loves her.

Believe for bigger and better. Not as it relates to fame, money, power, or status, but as it relates to what God can do in and through you. Take that step forward, and let God unfold the rest.

Is the dream you have big enough that you can reach it on your own? If so, it's probably too small. Consider not what you can do on your own, but map out a plan that can be accomplished only with God. Believe in a God-sized dream!

6

THIS IS THE DAY

Say Yes

Only a life lived for others is the life
worthwhile.

—Albert Einstein

L ife offers only few opportunities that are huge moments. Moments that happen unexpectedly and have a tremendous impact on the world around us. Moments when the need is great and the volunteers are few. If we don't step up and answer the call, we'll miss out on what God can do through us. It's important to be ready for these kinds of moments.

Show up when you can shine light on dark places. Be present whenever you can represent His love. Say yes, even if you feel tired, even if you're sick, and even if it seems inconvenient. Don't let these opportunities pass you by.

When Hurricane Irma started churning its way up the Atlantic Ocean in early September 2017, meteorologists were uncertain as to its impact. As it increased in size and power, the forecast started to look grim. Anticipating the storm to pose a severe threat to the entire state of Florida, Governor Rick Scott declared a state of emergency. Over the next several days, millions of Floridians left the state for safer ground. It was one of the largest evacuations in the history of the United States. Shelters across the state were waiting and ready to accommodate more than one hundred thousand residents.

As Irma decimated the island of Barbuda, it was clear this was no average hurricane. Maintaining a near-record wind speed of 185 miles per hour for a record thirty-seven hours, Irma was a destructive force in catastrophic proportions. And after leaving behind devastation in the Caribbean, it headed straight for Florida.

I'd been in communication with Governor Scott the weekend before the storm hit. He asked if I could help him deliver calls to action through social media, particularly as it concerned the special-needs shelters the government was preparing in advance of the storm. I jumped at the chance. I shot out messages on Facebook and Twitter. When I filmed *SportsCenter* and *SEC Nation* that weekend, I used the opportunity to do the same.

My original plan was to return to Atlanta after filming the ESPN and *SEC Nation* segments Saturday and then fly to Los Angeles on Sunday to train for baseball. Months earlier, I had scheduled this time to work with some of the top hitting coaches in the area. This was a big deal for me, a huge opportunity to improve and strengthen my game in the off-season. Not to mention something that had been on my calendar for a few months. The way I looked at it, it was possible the coming year would be my last chance to play professional sports. It was make or break time.

> If people around me are hurting, I don't want to go where it's safe. I want to bring hope.

At the same time, Hurricane Irma was on its way to slam my beloved home state. While no one knew exactly how bad or exactly which places in Florida were going to get hit the worst, most experts predicted a disaster in much of the state. A lot of people were telling me to go where it was safe. But I don't play safe. If people around me are hurting, I don't want to go where it's safe. I want to bring hope.

I wrestled with the decision a bit. The more I thought about it, however, the clearer my mind became. You don't get many opportunities to be in the state you grew up in and help your neighbors, near and far, in the midst of destruction. I could always get more time with hitting coaches, but I could never turn back time to do something for those whose lives could potentially be devastated for a long while. I knew the right thing to do. I hopped on a flight from Missouri and headed straight to my hometown of Jacksonville, Florida, to help prepare friends, family, and strangers for Irma's arrival.

Sunday morning, the hurricane breached the Florida coast. It roared through the Keys before raging its way up the Western Seaboard. The storm's devastating impact unfolded over the course of the next several days. Millions in sweltering heat were without power. Irma's powerful winds sucked ocean water out of bays. Record-breaking storm surges and flooding walloped parts of the state, including Jacksonville. Homes in the hardest hit neighborhoods were severely damaged or destroyed.

In the immediate wake of Irma's aftermath, I surveyed the damage in my neighborhood alone. No one had power. Trees were down all over yards; one of them had crashed through a friend's house. I rallied one of my best friends, Bryan, and a local police officer. Together we drove around flooded neighborhoods, making our way toward local shelters, seeing what we could do to help or bring some light and encouragement.

Two days after Hurricane Irma struck our state, I had the incredible opportunity to come alongside our governor and attend a hurricane briefing at the emergency operations center in Tallahassee. It was an honor to thank the couple hundred personnel there, including National Guard men and women, after their grueling week of managing preparation and response efforts.

I remember walking into a conference room where I would soon pray with some people. Noticing a Bible on the table, I pointed to it. "I like that book," I told the people in the room. "Good choice." After encouraging these hardworking men and women, I left with the governor to visit other parts of the state. Florida's adjutant general, Army Major General Michael Calhoun, who had met up with us that morning, joined us.

Over the course of the next several days, I traveled with the governor and, later and separately, Senator Marco Rubio, visiting shelters and outreach relief sites all over the state. I was honored to be able to accompany them on these trips. I get how polarizing politics can be for people, but this was bigger than politics. This was about helping people from the state I love.

GO TO THE STORMS

Under huge white tent canopies, over a hundred volunteers from the North Carolina Baptists on Mission (NCBM) hustled about helping those in need. This organization shuttled in equipment and volunteer teams to Florida a few days after Hurricane Irma struck. The teams would come in shifts and spend two or so weeks at a time until other relief volunteers took their place.

A group of men and women, most in their fifties and sixties and a few even in their seventies, set up a feeding unit in Big Pine Key. Some called it ground zero. NCBM set up a command center to organize their efforts. They were efficient, hardworking, and fast. These volunteers not only served ninety thousand meals each day to people in this region most severely affected by Irma but also offered cleanup crews. Hauling chain saws, they would cut down and clear out downed trees scattered throughout yards. And if someone needed help tearing out flood-soaked drywall and insulation, these people were there. Alongside Senator Rubio, I watched these North Carolinians in awe.

Wearing bright yellow T-shirts, each volunteer had a job. Some unloaded hundreds of pallets of bottled water. Some unpacked thousands and thousands of boxes containing food, utensils, take-out containers, and meal-prep supplies. Some cooked hot dogs and hamburgers in gigantic commercial-grade ovens. Some lined up behind long rectangular tables, spooning barbequed pork and fresh corn out of huge red buckets and into to-go boxes. Some manned the area where almost a hundred thousand people a day would wait in long lines in their cars, on foot, or on bikes looking for a hot meal, water, or a bag of ice.

As I helped serve some of these meals, I had the privilege of talking to the volunteers. They radiated joy. They loved serving. They were even enjoying themselves despite the oppressive heat. There's something about being on the front lines of a cause that blesses you in more ways than you can imagine. When I thanked them for all they were doing, they responded with wide smiles, saying things like "Well, we know we are serving for a greater purpose" and "Well, God served us first."

I noticed some of the volunteers wore hats with a bunch of different pins on them. Someone explained that each pin represented a hurricane, like Katrina, Matthew, and Harvey, where they had served to provide relief aid. Many of these volunteers had multiple pins on their hats, ten or twenty plus!

I talked to one man who had over twenty pins. He had to have been in his late sixties.

"In the last thirty years," he told me, "I was blessed to help out in all these places."

Another person with a bunch of pins told me, "Where there's a problem, I go."

"So it's your fault," I said. I immediately regretted my words. I didn't mean any offense by it, but it was probably too soon to make a joke.

Two-thirds of the state of Florida was without power and water, but thousands upon thousands were going to have a hot meal and water because of these volunteers. Even four weeks after the storm, the need was still great. Over six thousand meals per day were served.

I think about these fearless men and women volunteers. Most will not be known to the world. But these people were the hands and feet of Jesus in horrible catastrophes. They said yes when called and served with pleasure. Even if the world doesn't recognize their efforts, God sees what they do. And I know that one day they will be rewarded for it.

I met more amazing volunteers throughout the few days I traveled with Senator Rubio and Governor Scott after Hurricane Irma. I encouraged them as best I could, reminding them that what they were doing mattered. I prayed for them too and was more blessed when some of these incredible people prayed for me.

I think about what the one guy said: "Where there's a problem, I go." Is this something you do? When storms come, what's your initial reaction?

You may know that airplanes take off into the wind. You'd think it would make more sense for an aircraft to ascend with the wind behind it. However, that's not the case. Without my explaining the complex physics behind it, the fact is, flying into the wind actually reduces takeoff and landing distance.

A similar principle applies to eagles. An eagle is the only bird that loves storms. That's because it was created to rise above them. This magnificent creature has the unique ability to lock its wings in a fixed position. When it flies into a fierce storm, it will power on this natural mechanism and use the wind to soar above the storm. The eagle doesn't sit out the storm. It doesn't pretend it's not there. And it's not afraid of it. The eagle will fly straight into the storm.

Every one of us reacts differently when the storms of life come. Some try to escape them. Some use distractions to forget about them. Some do nothing and let themselves be whipped by driving rain and gusty wind.

Whatever we try to do to avoid a storm, one thing is for certain: it's there. It's unavoidable and impossible to ignore. Here's the thing: As believers, we have the knowledge, the powerful truth, that we can overcome every storm with God. And when the storms hit those around us, like an airplane or an eagle flying into the wind, we need to rise up. We need to lean into the chaos.

We need to realize the world is full of hurting people. And because we are followers of Jesus, we can bring people out of the storms of life. We can help heal the broken. We can help bring hope where there looks to be none. We can show love where little, if any, exists.

You may never experience a natural disaster like Hurricane Irma in your lifetime. I certainly hope that's the case. But you will surely endure a crisis or a trial or know someone who will. Don't walk away from or numb yourself through it. Recognize this as an opportunity to show Jesus and share about a hope that is greater than anything else.

Say yes and serve as His hands and His feet. When you do this, you open yourself to the possibility of doing something meaningful that will change lives, something that probably won't happen if you spend all your free time bingeing on Netflix. Getting off the couch, flying into a storm, and helping bring others out of it will change people's lives. Like the eagle that locks its wings, lock arms with those in need and rise above.

THE NEED IS GREAT

Day after day that week, I visited shelters and relief stations all over Florida. All I wanted to do was reach out to people and make them feel loved. It's not like anyone necessarily needed me to hand out a bottle of water or a meal, though I was happy to do that. There were plenty of volunteers. And it's not like I could do as much as the governor or the senator. I certainly don't have their kind of power. I simply wanted to reach out to people and tell them they are loved. I wanted to show them they mattered. I wanted to pray with them, bring them hope after losing their possessions and even their homes.

When you know you are not alone, when you know others are fighting a battle alongside you, it makes things a little more bearable. These evacuees were dealing with a lot—a lot of worry, a lot of doubt, a lot of unknown. But if there was a chance just to brighten their day for a couple of seconds or minutes, it was worth it. I couldn't promise them the moon, and it's not easy to find the right words to say to encourage someone, but I could hopefully put a smile on their faces.

I'll never forget one of the first few shelters I visited that welcomed hundreds of people who had nowhere to go. On one hand, I was warmed by the generosity of volunteers and National Guard men and women. On the other hand, it was heartbreaking to see entire families huddled up on mats on a gymnasium floor, their most precious belongings packed up in boxes or duffle bags next to them.

As I walked around handing out water and supplies, I noticed an African American boy, ten or eleven years old, walk toward me. He stood right in front of me and put his arms around one of my legs. Tears started rolling down his cheeks. I knelt down on the ground to hug the boy. His name was Joshua. He kept saying, "Tim, you are my hero. I can't believe you are here." And I kept telling him, "God has an awesome plan for your life, Joshua. Keep being a fighter. Keep being strong for your family."

Joshua followed me around the entire time I was there. As I was about to leave with the governor, I turned down a hallway and looked back. Joshua stood thirty feet away. Big, sad tears fell down his face. I hated having to leave him. I walked back and gave him a long hug. I promised to keep in touch.

In another shelter, I was approached by a guy in his late fifties. His face was hardened, with sun-leathered skin and haunted eyes. He was dressed in a faded and ripped tank top. From an external first impression, it was easy to imagine he'd had a rough life.

When this man said hello, his cheeks were wet with tears. "You're a real Christian, aren't you? Will you pray for my mom and dad?"

"Of course," I said. "What are your parents' names?"

He told me and I replied, "How about we do one better? How about we find somewhere it's quiet and I'll pray for them right now?"

We walked over to the other side of the gymnasium, and he wrapped his arm around me. I prayed for this man, for his future, for the plan God had for his life, and for his parents.

I remember walking into a special-needs shelter that accommodated primarily the elderly who were sick. I met more amazing people as I walked around the open space packed with cots and said hello to each person.

Before I left, I knelt beside a white-haired vet who may have been in his eighties. He lay on a cot, propped up by some pillows and covered with a thick wool blanket. A fluffy dog sat on his lap. This man and I talked a bit. Then to everyone's delight, especially mine, he whipped out a harmonica and played a cool tune. When he was finished, he broke out in a toothless grin. My smile was just as big. This man had served our country and made incredible sacrifices for us. I hope we can do the same for him.

In that same shelter, a woman in her fifties approached me and begged me to see her mother (it may have been her grandmother, I can't remember). "Of course," I said. She grabbed my hand and led me to an area that was sectioned off. There, individual cots were partitioned by bedsheets to provide more privacy for evacuees who had severe health issues.

As I walked inside one such space, I saw an elderly woman, probably in her nineties, lying on a cot. Her face was drained of color, and her mouth was open. She sucked in shallow, raspy breaths. I knelt beside this emaciated woman and stroked her wispy white hair. She was trying to say something, but I couldn't understand her. She just kept smiling. Her daughter looked on, laughing and saying, "Oh, look how happy Mom is. It doesn't seem real, does it?" I just smiled and held this woman's hand. Over and over, I told her Jesus loves her. This smiling woman's name was Irma.

When I was helping out with the North Carolina Baptists on Mission, I remember a car pulling up to the feeding unit. I stuck my head in the passenger window and said, "Hi! How many meals do you need?"

The driver looked at me and exclaimed, "Hey, you're Tim Tebow."

"Yes, I am, sir. What's your name?"

He told me his name, then added, "I'm a pastor of a church down the street."

"That's awesome, sir. How's your church?"

He shook his head and sighed. "It's wiped out."

"I am so sorry." We talked more and then, after recognizing a familiar accent, I asked him, "Where are you from?"

"The Philippines," he said.

"Me too! I was born in the Makati Medical Center, right outside Manila."

Tears started flowing down the man's face. "Thank you so much for what you do for our people and for helping out here in Florida."

Horns started blaring behind this guy. We were holding up the line. I hugged him goodbye. As this man drove off, I thought how neat it is when we discover a connection with someone else. This happens when we pause and take the time to talk to people and get to know them, even just a little bit. A certain camaraderie comes out of that, a needed reminder that we're on the same team. That we're rooting for each other. That we need each other. That we want to help each other. There's something special about that.

Meeting volunteers from so many churches, organizations like the Red Cross, and men and women serving in the National Guard blessed me beyond measure. Their sacrifice does not go unnoticed. And, oh, these amazing men, women, and children of Florida who endured through Hurricane Irma! How powerful it is to see people who have lost much show such strength and resilience. They were such an encouragement to me.

LEAN IN

When obstacles come and crises hit, we can step up and do something that matters. In Irma's aftermath, I saw thousands and thousands of volunteers—I like to call them heroes—who on an ordinary day might not get the chance to give so selflessly. They were more than just human beings. Rallying with one another, in spite of whatever differences they may have had, these people were rescue teams, helping families escape flood-ravaged neighborhoods. They were food and water teams, providing those without electricity and power something to eat. They were Jesus-giving teams, encouraging those who had nowhere to go. This is powerful.

As Christians, we have to be aware of the world around us. We have to take the focus off ourselves and our problems and do something for someone else. Not only is doing this part of our identity in Jesus, but it also helps to put things in perspective. I think some people are waiting for this crazy revolution, a mind-blowing revelation, or some big event like a natural disaster to step up and show the love of Jesus. During a natural disaster, sure, it's easy to see the need. But I've learned that opportunities are plentiful every day, sometimes right in front of our eyes—in our own communities, even in our own families.

We just need to be ready to say yes.

We need to infiltrate the places that desperately need the hope of God. We need to be in the hospitals, homeless shelters, orphanages, and homes down the street or across town. You don't have to be skilled at carpentry, have a medical background, or know how to use a commercial-grade oven to help another person. When you use what you've got, knowing God's hand is in it, you can bring light wherever you go.

Recently, I spoke at Aggie Stadium in Albertville, Alabama. About ten thousand people showed up. Most were students from a total of twelve local middle and high schools, plus some parents and others. I learned on the way there that a young girl had overdosed on drugs that weekend. It was a heartbreaking time for the community.

Before the event began, I spent time with a bunch of Night to Shine guests and their families. When I walked into the room, my eyes fell on a girl in a wheelchair. She covered her face and started crying when I gave her a hug. Her tears were contagious. I was so happy to see her, to love on her. I held this precious girl for a solid minute.

Then I met a young man named Gabe. His bright smile lit up the room, and his spirit was even more dynamic. I could just tell he was a fighter. Gabe had no legs and only one arm, but he was determined to live a full life.

It was like this for a while, meeting incredible people who were overcoming challenges most of us can't even fathom facing. Every hug I received, every smile that beamed my way, every conversation I had pumped me up. I spent way too long in this room, but I only know that because the organizer of the event had to pull me out as I was dreadfully late for my talk.

Now, as fired up as I was, I realized in that moment, I wasn't totally prepared to speak. Understand this: I'm the type of person who can't fully prepare a message until I get to the venue. Prior to this, I pray about what I'm going to say and create a rough outline. But in order to fully craft a talk, it's important that I get a feel for the environment, the pulse of the crowd, their hearts, their stories. These things have a tremendous impact on my message.

I usually have enough time to figure this out. In this particular event, however, everything happened so fast. The minute someone hustled me out of this room to get on stage, I barely had enough time to grab a water on my way out. Then I was rushed straight to the platform to talk. I didn't even have a few minutes to think while someone was introducing me. It was all a bit disorienting.

Fifteen minutes into my talk, I started getting disappointed with myself. I didn't think what I was saying was coming across powerfully. My talk was missing something. It was frustrating. I remember staring into the crowd of ten thousand people, seeing some of the same ones with special needs that I had talked to earlier. They weren't the only ones out there. I saw hundreds of people—young, old, male, female—who had physical disabilities or suffered from serious medical conditions. I wanted so desperately to give them hope in my message, but felt I was failing miserably.

And then, at that fifteen-minute mark, God took over my babble. I felt Him saying, "Timmy, remember why you are here. It's not about how fancy your words are or how great you sound. It's about having a heart for these people like I do." In other words, I had to step aside.

When we think we have power in our words alone, they will fall flat. If God's power is in us and speaks through us, however, the words we speak will never fail. I ended the talk by giving an invitation to anyone who wanted to trust in Jesus. Hundreds walked over to a small building on the side where many volunteers were waiting to pray with and encourage them.

On the way back home, I wrote this down: *I went into this event knowing God but trusting myself instead of knowing myself and trusting God.* When I remembered the message wasn't about me, He took my average ability and my pride and brought so many people to Him. We serve a big God who will use even what stands in our way, whether our faults or our insecurities, and turn it around for His glory. That's how great He is!

Yes!

MAKE THIS YOUR DAY

Do you approach each day with confidence, knowing that someone's life can be eternally changed because of what you shared with or did for that person? Do you live emboldened with courage, knowing that you can impact a situation for good because of whose you are? Do you rise above your fears, knowing that no matter what you face or how bad you may feel, as a child of God you are more than a conqueror (see Romans 8:37, NIV)?

When you live out what it means to be a son or daughter of God, you can do great things. Things that matter, things that are significant. You can change lives. You can make a difference. You can have the courage to say yes.

What is something that holds you back from stepping up and saying yes? How can you overcome this obstacle?

7

THIS IS THE DAY

Put in the Work

The comfort zone is one of the greatest enemies of human potential. When people get into a comfort zone, they strive to stay in that comfort zone. . . . You need the courage to continually move yourself in the direction of your biggest goals and ambitions. You need to be willing to face discomfort in order for you to grow.

—Brian Tracy

The race is not always won by the fastest runner. A day is not always conquered by the one who has the most skill, the most smarts, the most talent, or the most money. The one who tries to live each day to its potential is the one who doesn't give up. She's the one who is not afraid of working hard for something that matters. He's the one who doesn't let setbacks stop his momentum. She's the one who is not afraid of the pain of growth. He's the one who will fight no matter how big or strong his opponent.

You know I'm a pretty competitive guy. What you might not know is that this trait runs deep in my family. In fact, we are equally, freakishly competitive. Put my family in a room by ourselves and it's like a pen of angry guard dogs. Someone's going to get bitten. It doesn't matter if we're playing Mafia or dodgeball or debating a political issue, we will each fight to our death to win or be right. Let me tell you a story so you can see what I mean.

It was the day we'd all been waiting for. Each member of my family, as well as some close friends and their significant others, woke up on our first morning of vacation together to the sound of blaring alarms. No one would snooze. No one would oversleep.

Rise and shine, Tebow family. It's time for Beach Olympics.

We all prepared for the events differently. A few stretched. Some gulped an extra cup of coffee, others a protein shake. We were all getting ready to crush . . . each other. Did I mention this was our first full day of vacation?

Vacations for most mean a lot of doing nothing. At times, this is great. Hey, we could all use some down time. But since I had planned this trip, I figured I'd do it Tebow style. For us, there's no better way to get our blood pumping, adrenaline rushing, and hearts racing like good ole competition.

Another thing: I knew that this particular year I wasn't going to have a ton of extra time to spend with my family and close friends. So it was most important to hang out together as a group. I find what happens on most vacations is that everyone wants to do their own things. Some take off on walks for hours, while others prefer to relax by the pool or go snorkeling. Before you know it, vacation is over and it's time to go home and not everyone had the chance to really connect with one another. Organizing special activities for us to enjoy was a surefire way to be together.

The goal for the first few days was to participate in super fun activities, summer-camp style. These included physical events like Beach Olympics and mental ones like Trivia. Then we'd have a few days when everyone could relax and do whatever he or she wanted.

The more I thought through the planning process with my assistant, Anne, the more I realized it made sense to start each day with one such event—you know, before everyone rushed off to bake in the sun or swim in the ocean. One day, I arranged a paddleboard race. Another, a road-cart relay. The next, a snake-wrangling contest. Seriously, I'm not kidding—a special visit from a huge albino python had been scheduled for that morning. This white snake, colored with patterns of butterscotch yellow, was thicker than a baseball bat and measured over twelve feet long. The goal was to wrangle this scaly creature from head to tip into a large burlap sack. I'd like to tell you I won this event, but I didn't. I will say that the most impressive competitor in the event was my sister Christy. She was the only girl in our group who participated. Man, her courage was inspiring. Everyone was rooting for her!

> Right before my eyes, I saw her foot swell up like a balloon.

Back to Beach Olympics. In our first event, Minesweeper, my mom, who happens to be the sweetest lady in the world, got hurt. Right before my eyes, I saw her foot swell up like a balloon. It started turning different shades of black and blue. It looked painful, outright nasty.

Unless you actually saw her foot, you'd never know Mom was injured. She wasn't going to let what was broken or sprained and turning every color of a mood ring stop her. There were prizes to win, like plastic gold medals. Not to mention the sweet taste of victory from coming in first. Mom plodded along like a champ. She limped as fast as she could, weaving through obstacle courses with remarkable grit.

Man, I felt so bad for her. At one point while we were all taking a break, I pulled her aside and said, "Mom, please stop. You don't have to do this." She basically just rolled her eyes and said, "Timmy, please," while walking (or trying to) away. We're talking about the woman who gave birth to us five. You can see where our competitiveness comes from.

During Tug of War, when I saw her dig her bloated foot, which looked nothing like a foot at this point, into the sand with unrelenting determination,

I broke. I stood behind her, my arm wrapped around her waist so she wouldn't bear any of the weight on what we learned later was in fact a broken foot.

As soon as my siblings on the opposing team noticed what I had done, they flipped out.

"You're cheating!"

"C'mon, that's not fair!"

"Put her down! Put her down now!"

Even Mom's injury didn't warrant her a get-out-of-jail-free card.

I'm not super proud to admit this, but the last couple of events during Beach Olympics escalated to an ugly level. One person was such a sore loser, he (or she) refused to speak to the person that beat him (or her). Someone almost got into a fight with another person who, gunning for first place, accidentally rammed someone's canoe into my father's ribcage. I apparently ticked off a good friend who was so angry with my smack talk, he stormed back to his hotel room.

It didn't take long for us to start attracting curious onlookers. At one point, some guy in his early twenties walked up to my sister Katie, who was standing a few feet away from Robby and me. I couldn't hear what they were talking about, but their facial expressions piqued my interest.

Five minutes later Katie, her eyes lit like a firecracker, ran over to my brother and me. Pointing her thumb at the guy she was just talking to, our sister told us he was part of a family reunion, and in a matter of minutes a bunch of their crew, including college football and basketball players, as well as some West Point grads, would be swarming the beach.

Katie blurted with excitement, "He wants to challenge us!" Then her eyes darkened. I knew the look well. "He even said they would crush us at anything."

Fighting words. Music to the Tebows' ears.

Turned out, this party had checked in early that morning. The timing couldn't have been better. We were all so fired up from Beach Olympics, we needed to reroute some of that fierce energy. Or, at least, get it off each other. It was time to push aside our differences and rally together.

An hour or so later, Team Tebow stared down our opposing team, a gang of six-feet-plus guys, shredded and looking like actual Olympic contenders. But we were ready. We were going to do whatever it took to win. Before we got started, both teams made a bet. If our team lost, we'd donate one thousand dollars to a charity of the other team's choosing, the Wounded Warrior Project. If they lost, they would donate the same amount of money to the Tim Tebow Foundation.

We had six people on our team, four men and two women. They had six guys. Without boring you to death with the complicated rules and regulations, think of it as dodgeball on a sand volleyball court. The game lasted four minutes. In case you skipped over that last part, I'll say it again. The game lasted *four minutes*. Oh yeah, and when we won, every single person on our team was still standing. We rallied strong. We locked in. We pushed ourselves to the max.

The next game was Danney Ball, which is volleyball using a ten-pound medicine ball. Apparently, the guy who approached Katie had seen us playing it earlier that morning—it was a great way for me to get in a workout on vacation. "Let's play that game," he had told her, and added with an arrogant grin, "It doesn't look that hard."

It was supposed to be two on two, but we played three players against their six. Drenched with sweat and stained with sand, we grunted, spiked, and dove our way to game point, 13–2. Right before one of us on Team Tebow was about to lob the weighted ball over in a serve, the other team started whining about something or other. Finally, in a bit of a cocky move and to get these meatheads to stop being babies, I offered to switch scores. "Your serve," I said, granting them possession of the ball. And just like that, we accepted the losing score, 2–13.

I almost think this gave us an edge. It forced us to work harder, power through with every ounce of strength we had to give. After a few minutes of sweat, blood, and tears on our end, working through pain and fatigue, we crushed them, 15–13.

Now, the guys we were playing against were strong. Real strong. And while we on Team Tebow were strong as well, we were also born competitors. We had stamina. We could push through pain. We could endure through discomfort. Fall down five times, get up six.

These characteristics go beyond vacation competitions. It's a spirit you need in life!

Want to get better at something?

Want to be successful?

Want to see that dream happen?

Want to make a difference?

Want to conquer life's obstacles, detours, and sucker punches?

You need grit. You need drive. You need to be persistent. You need to work hard. You need to change. You need to grow. You need these things to give whatever passion you have momentum.

MAKE IT COUNT

When I was about five years old, my nickname was Shade Tree. It wasn't a good thing. I'll explain.

Because we lived on a forty-acre farm, we kids had a long chore list. There was always something to do. Mow lawns. Chop wood. Chase cows into the fields. Lift bales of hay. Weed the garden.

My siblings worked hard. They tackled their chores with gusto. I, however, did not. In my defense, I was only five.

One of my first jobs was to rake the dirt into rows in the garden. Easy enough. I'm sure my parents didn't expect me to do it perfectly, but they had some expectations. For the first two months, I remember that instead of doing my chore, I'd stand on the rake wearing this huge camouflage-colored hat. So while my siblings, dripping with sweat, chopped wood, weeded the garden, and lifted bales of hay, I just stood there. Hence the nickname Shade Tree.

After a few days of watching my siblings hard at work, I started realizing something. Hard work pays off. Things actually get done. When that light bulb clicked on, I started working circles around my brothers and sisters. I did more than just rake dirt. I filled their buckets with water. I fed the cows. I even helped carry bales of hay. I started to build the work ethic I have today.

> Many people want the rewards of hard work, but few are willing to put in the effort.

Now, I've never believed in working hard for the sole sake of working hard. It's always been important for me to strive for something that matters. And hard work gives you the best chance at reaching that goal. Many people want the rewards of hard work, but few are willing to put in the effort required to reap the end result.

I remember a conversation I had with one of my teammates in baseball who happened to be a good friend. One day, I pulled him aside in private. I wanted to encourage him but also tell him something he needed to hear, not necessarily something he wanted to hear. I said, "You are one of the best players on the team. You are so gifted. You can hit for power. You have incredible skill. But you are not even coming close to reaching your potential." I told him if he wanted to get to the bigs and make the most of his talent, he needed to consider changing his diet. He needed to fuel his body better. Eat more protein and less sugar. Quit the soft drinks and drink more water.

Striving to get better at anything takes discipline. You've got to live sore. You've got to live uncomfortable. You've got to make sacrifices. You may hurt today, but you'll be better for it tomorrow.

One of my teammates I played with years ago was born with incredible athleticism. He was a good dude who did great things on the field. Problem was, he was unwilling to put in the work because it hurt. It was painful. It made him uncomfortable and exhausted. Despite being one of the most talented guys I've ever played with, he ended up not doing anything in professional sports. I wonder what he would be doing today had he locked in and put in the work—and pushed through the pain.

Growing up, I tacked a quote on my bedroom wall that said, *Somewhere he is out there training while I am not, and when we meet, he will win.* I got this from a commercial I watched as a boy in the nineties. It showed little kids around the world shooting free throws into hoops. This statement spoke volumes to me. It inspired me to get up and do something when someone else wasn't.

I believe in becoming your best in whatever you do. Whether as an athlete, a parent, a business owner, an actor, a doctor, a police officer, a student—anything. As Christians, we are taught to do life in word and action to the glory of God. Working hard at being your best, making the most out of whatever He has given or called you to do, is a way to thank God for this day.

In sports, for me this means I'm going to show up an hour or two before practice. I'm going to get in two hundred more swings or ten extra reps, or run an extra mile, or train on my off day. Someone might be stronger or faster than me, but this day, I'm going to gain ground.

When I was at the University of Florida, our whole college program was centered on bringing out our mental toughness. Obviously, we focused on speed and strength, but it was secondary to the goal of developing grit. I remember how each day a list was posted on the board of the hardest workers on the whole team, listed in order from players one to a hundred. I was number one every day my entire four years at school. Except for one day. I think whoever did that probably just wanted to tick me off.

Pain Can Be Good

Growth can be painful. It means getting out of your comfort zone. It means getting inconvenienced. But if you don't grow, you don't change. And if you don't change, you stay stuck.

The Bible talks about how we start off in our spiritual journey as babies living on milk (see Hebrews 5:13), but we must grow up so we can eat solid food. Pain, for the most part, is not our enemy. It's a sign of growth. It's evidence of maturity.

I was always willing to put my body on the line and accept the pain so I could reap the reward. There were times when I was running drills for football that I'd think my legs were going to explode or fall off. It was tempting to give in to the pain and quit—it's not like I hadn't already pushed myself beyond my limit. But I remember thinking, *It's okay. I'd rather run around this stadium with my legs on fire and be the first one to finish.* I think back to the few times I could have given just one more rep or a few extra seconds, but didn't. The regret would haunt me for days.

If you are looking for a feel-good self-help book, you should probably stop reading right now. Because here's the thing: Striving for something and living a life of significance doesn't always feel good. Sometimes it hurts. Sometimes it's uncomfortable. Sometimes it's outright painful. You have to do the hard things to get to where you need to go. My goal in life is not to be comfortable. It's to push my limits. It's to fight for something, no matter the cost.

I remember playing with the Broncos against the Patriots the night in January 2012 when the windchill fell below zero. We were getting slaughtered by New England. Shortly into the third quarter, we were down 42–7. I'll never forget getting tackled and hitting the ground, crushed by the weight of five or six Patriots piling on top of me. On impact, I felt my chest snap. I'd find out later I had broken multiple bones in my chest that were connected to my sternum. It was a whole bunch of ridiculousness. When I got up, I could feel the broken bones shifting and popping. The pain was excruciating. This was a chance for me to make a statement for my team. See, it's not just about showing up when you're winning. It's about rallying when you're getting blown out and there is no probable chance of a comeback. I played the rest of the game. Every single snap. Now, I admit staying in the game probably made my injuries worse, but I was determined to stick it out and fight. If I'm going down, I'm going to go down fighting.

You don't need to break some bones to push through pain. Sometimes it's just about getting uncomfortable to do what's right or what matters. I strive hard to impact others for good. I want to show people I truly care.

As I was writing these words this past weekend, I reorganized my schedule and changed around a few different flights just so I could stay an hour longer in Atlanta to watch the first half of my niece's soccer game. Now, I love my nieces and nephews, and I love spending time with them. But the fact is, watching a bunch of kids run after a soccer ball is not necessarily my favorite thing in the world to do. Knowing how much my watching the game would mean to my niece, however, was worth every change I had to make.

I think about my transition from football to baseball. Talk about tough, real tough. And talk about needing to grow and change and improve. I had spent over a decade training a certain way and honing certain skills, and suddenly, I had to drop everything I'd learned to train a different way for a sport I hadn't played in ten years. In many respects, I was at a disadvantage. I was driven by this sense of urgency trying to make up for lost time. I had to focus on training in a new way, figuring out what I had to do to excel in baseball, and then do it. I had to figure out my edge and work on it to be at my very best. I'm still doing this. It's part of the process.

Growth Takes Time

Many people want instant gratification. They don't want to invest the time it takes to develop relationships, a work ethic, or long-term success in anything. Wanting the perfect body means getting surgery or starving instead of tweaking eating habits and getting exercise. Wanting a fancy car or a big house means borrowing money instead of waiting and saving. Wanting the high grade means cheating instead of studying. Work ethic today is underrated. Many people want to go from A to Z without taking any steps in between.

> We've created a society that has made people famous for doing nothing.

It seems like today it's easier than ever to be famous. How many people post a video on YouTube or Instagram, hoping it'll go viral, and if it does—boom!—they're instant celebrities. Probably more than you think. I'm not knocking social media or reality TV, but these things often become a way to

THIS IS THE DAY

gain instant fame. We don't care how good our music is; we just care how many people listen to it. We don't care how good our performance is; we just want everyone to come see the show. We've created a society that has made people famous for doing nothing because it's so easy!

And this is what makes the grind of life, the hard work, the tireless pursuit of excellence, the countless hours of practice behind the scenes, the attempts, the fails, and the restarts unattractive. Sure, there are plenty of people who will reach their goals by skipping steps. But learning how to face and work through the grind gives you the greatest potential of being everything you can be. I never set out to work the hardest in whatever I did. I just never wanted to regret not being the best I could be by not giving it my all.

There is no instant payoff with growth. It's not like I train for an hour and see results the next day. I train, and guess what happens next? I hurt. I'm uncomfortable. Sometimes I'm even in pain. The payoff is in the faith that the training will pay off. I recover and I get better. And then I repeat the cycle over and over and over again.

KEEP AT IT

I'm a pretty persistent guy. Having a fierce, competitive nature, I don't give up easily. I admire this quality in others. Which reminds me of a story.

After playing a game when I was with the Port St. Lucie Mets, I headed to the locker room. It was time to shower, change, and hop back on a bus to a motel or our next destination.

As I got closer to my locker, I noticed a young man standing right next to my stuff. He looked my age, maybe a few years younger. I assumed he was one of the clubbies who work for our team. These guys help with things like preparing the water coolers, feeding the players, washing the uniforms, getting baseballs ready, and so on. I didn't think much of it, so I just went about my business.

"What's up, man?" I said, while digging into my locker to grab some clean socks.

"Hello," he replied, nodding and smiling. A minute passed. He was still standing by my locker.

Strange. I had a strong feeling this dude was not a clubbie. "Can I help you with something?" I asked.

It was like the guy let out all the breath he'd been holding. "Oh man," he gushed. "It's so nice to meet you. My name is such-and-such. I can't believe I'm actually right here with you. Oh my goodness. Wow!"

"Nice to meet you too," I said while thinking, *Who is this guy? And what is he doing in here?*

I didn't want to spook him, so I tried to act nonchalant. "So," I said, while unlacing my cleat, "do you need something, man?"

Still standing, still staring, and still smiling, the dude answered, "No. I just wanted to meet you."

"All right, cool. Uh, so are you supposed to be in here?"

"No."

By now, some of my teammates had taken notice of this guy. They started making funny gestures at me. I didn't know what to do, other than to keep talking to him.

"So how did you get in?" I asked.

"I broke in," the guy blurted out, almost apologetically.

My buddies started howling in the background.

"Uh, okay. So how did you do that?"

"Well, I was in the back for a while, and then I just waited until the coast was clear. Then I hopped the fence and walked in after the last of the security people left. The door to the locker room was locked, so I just figured out how to get it open."

I didn't know what to say. At that point, I was thinking that calling security wouldn't have been a terrible idea.

As he stood and stared, his grin stretched wide, I said, "Well, uh, I appreciate your determination. You got at least one good quality that I know of."

Suddenly, the smile faded. "Please don't rat me out," he begged.

Turns out, someone had notified security, and before I could say anything else, the guy ran out of the locker room. He was pretty fast. I found out later he was chased down by a police officer and questioned.

Here's the deal: persistence is important. While I'm not saying what this guy did was right, he was willing to push through whatever obstacles stood in his way—in his case, a fence and a locked door.

What are you willing to climb over, hustle around, or break through to make something happen? In your marriage . . . your family . . . your dream . . . your relationship with God? Whatever your goal is, don't give up. Keep at it.

BE THE EXAMPLE OTHERS WILL FOLLOW

When I was a sophomore, I transferred to Nease High School to play football. New to the team, I had quite an impression to make. I wanted to prove I was the best. I also wanted to change the culture of a team that was known for being everyone's homecoming game. I wanted to be the example of what it meant to have heart, character, and fight.

Near the end of my first season with the team, we faced off against Pedro Menendez High School. At the end of the first quarter, we were already getting demolished, 17–0. After I was throwing on the run, I planted my right foot underneath me and one of the defenders hit me low. I heard a sickening crunch. My right leg snapped. Red-hot pain surged through me as I hobbled to the sideline. Coach Craig Howard asked if I was all right.

"Yeah, I'm fine," I replied, blinking to try and clear the haze of pain.

"Well, good. 'Cause we've got a game to win. Son, we're down seventeen to nothing. This is the stuff legends are made out of. Now get back in there!"

I jogged back on the field and fought hard, trying to compensate with my good leg for the bum one. The limp I was playing with got worse with every passing quarter. Whenever the pain would start to compromise my game, I'd remember Coach Howard's words: "This is the stuff legends are made out of."

It wasn't about winning the game. It was about my teammates. It was about the team. It was about trying to change our reputation of being soft. If I wanted to be a leader, I had to act like one. I had to build the respect of my teammates. I couldn't think of a better way to do that than to play on a broken leg.

I'll never forget at the end of the fourth quarter running twenty yards toward the end zone. A safety was gunning for me. He came in from an angle, and his angle met mine on the one-yard line to the tune of a nasty collision. I got the touchdown, but he broke his leg. On a high note—for our team, at least—Nease evened the score 24–24.

When Menendez won the game 27–24 with a winning field goal, my heart sank. I remember limping toward my parents on the sideline. I hurt so bad, I could barely stand. Knowing there was only one more game in the season and I wouldn't be able to play due to my broken leg, I cried.

The worst thing about getting injured is not necessarily the pain of the injury but the pain of what the injury will cost. It's the pain of what you will miss out on. The pain of wondering if someone is going to get a jump on you while you rehab. Yeah, I hurt. But the disappointment of not being able to play was worse. I determined to come back stronger and faster after sitting out the rest of the season.

You don't get a lot of moments in life to prove yourself, but in that game I was given that chance. It was the first time in ten years that the school had a break-even season. The next year was even better. More people wanted to try out for the team. More players bought into the mentality that working hard would pay off. More teammates showed up in the weight room. And in our senior year, we won our first-ever state championship.

If you want to create change and influence others, you need to earn their respect. You do this not only by loving them, treating them with kindness, and not being judgmental but also by being committed. By showing them what it means to give your all, not just with words but in action. Do more than just talk.

Ultimately, life is based on a bunch of choices. The most important decision you'll ever make is to say yes to trusting Jesus. Going forward, you must decide what to do with whatever He puts on your heart or asks of you. Maybe you feel nudged to take a mission trip. Or start a business. Or go back to school. Or take better care of your health. Or spend more time with your loved ones. When you are pursuing a desire you feel God has given you, it's important to put in the work.

Some people believe that you're either born with a solid work ethic or you're not. I believe it's based on choices. It's about making the choice to say yes to the right things over and over and over again. You may not feel like it. It might be hard. It might require some pain. But you do it, and you don't stop doing it.

Make up your mind to do whatever is before you as best as you can. Focus on these priorities, and don't get anxious about the result. You don't have to reach your goal or your dream overnight. Actually, you probably won't.

And one last thing: don't get sidetracked if you experience a setback or stumble from time to time. It happens. It might happen again. Resolve to get up, take another swing, and keep at it.

MAKE THIS YOUR DAY

There are areas in most of our lives where we can do better, reset our habits, or improve in some way. This will require us to dig deep, embrace the grind, and work hard. We may not be able to change our circumstances, but we can learn and grow and develop our character from our experience. We don't have to give up after failure; we can determine to find a way to make something work.

And that's the key word—*work*.

> What are you willing to do spiritually, emotionally, physically, or mentally—or all these things—to get better, to get back up, to try something new, to take a risk, to get out of a familiar and comfortable space, to reach for something you believe God is calling you to do? Are you willing to do the work—and endure?

8

THIS IS THE DAY

Open Your Eyes

Wherever you are, be all there!

—Jim Elliot

had no idea if we were going to make it to the airport on time. I had just finished doing some publicity in New York City for my second book, *Shaken,* and had little over an hour to catch a flight to Atlanta. After snaking through Manhattan's city streets, the taxi tore down the New Jersey Turnpike headed to Newark Airport.

When the cab pulled to the curb at the terminal, my assistant, Anne, and I practically dove out of the car. The airport was buzzing with activity during rush hour in the middle of the Christmas season. Through the glass window, I could see the terminal was flooded with passengers, so I opted to check in outside. Fumbling through her handbag for her ID, Anne answered questions that a man behind the check-in counter fired at her. As I heaved the luggage onto the weight scale, I noticed an old, beat-up car pull up by the curb nearby. Bleary-eyed and rushed travelers were emerging from fifty different sloppily parked cars, and I happened to be drawn to that one.

A young woman, pale, in her early twenties tops, got out of the vehicle. She looked unsure, scared. Her clothes hung on her small frame, her bulging backpack old and tattered. The driver and another young man, both around her age, stepped out of the car to give her awkward half hugs and spout off goodbyes. Then the car sped off. The young woman stood glued to the sidewalk, eyes darting in all directions. It seemed she didn't have a clue what to do. I wondered if this was her first time traveling by plane. *What's going on with her?* I thought.

Before this trip, I'd been thinking how most of us fill our days with ceaseless activities that leave us little room to even catch our breath. Often, we are so consumed with where we're going, we barely give the process of getting there any thought. I'd been learning at the time that while the destination is important, we can have just as much impact on the actual journey. We don't have to be so singularly focused that we become blind to or ignore the people around us, even strangers that may cross our path.

After check-in and learning our flight was delayed, we were ready to go inside the terminal. That's when I noticed that the young woman was still planted near the curb, fumbling nervously with her backpack. She hadn't moved but an inch or two from where I first saw her.

I turned to Anne and pointed discreetly toward the lady. "See that girl over there? I don't know what it is, but I think she needs help. Why don't you go over and see if you can encourage or help her or something?"

"Of course," Anne said with a nod and began to walk toward the woman.

I headed inside and watched through the glass window as Anne and this woman spoke briefly. Bouncing her attention from the woman to the man behind the counter, Anne appeared to be helping this woman check in to her flight. Then Anne rushed back into the terminal.

"Her name is Amber," she told me. "She's traveling alone for the first time and doesn't have any idea what to do. Also, she's going to Tennessee, but her first flight arrives in Atlanta, the same one we're on." *Divine appointment?* I wondered.

It didn't feel right to leave Amber on her own. "Have her come with us," I offered.

When Anne came back inside the terminal with Amber, I introduced myself. Amber said hello in a shaky voice. She seemed shy, mistrustful of our offer to help. It's sad we live in a society where unexpected kindness is often met with suspicion.

The three of us chatted while we walked toward security. Just small talk, nothing too deep. As we approached an expressionless TSA agent checking IDs and boarding passes, Amber hesitated. The agent barked for her to hurry up. Passengers behind us groaned. Hands trembling, this woman was getting visibly flustered.

I spoke quietly and calmly. "Okay, Amber. Just take out your identification."

She nodded, wobbly fingers digging into her pocket for her driver's license.

"Now take out your boarding pass."

For those of us who fly frequently and are accustomed to the hustle of security lines, it's easy to forget how overwhelming this process can be for a newbie. When the agent waved us off into the long line of passengers removing shoes and whipping off belts, I helped Amber make sure everything went in the correct bins and down the conveyer belt. We finally broke through the

THIS IS THE DAY

other side. With some time to kill, we all headed toward the Delta lounge to grab a bite to eat.

We chowed down and talked, hearing the details of Amber's story. What we learned from the bits she told us at the time was heartbreaking. She had recently broken up with her boyfriend. It didn't end well. Details aside, there were lies, betrayal, abuse, and abandonment. The man she was once madly in love with had kicked her out of what she called home and into the streets. Homeless, she slept wherever she could. She'd spent a few nights at a local police station. The officers came to know her by name. Every now and then, a friend would pay for a night at some motel where she could take a hot shower and sleep in a warm bed. Amber got so sick at one point, she had to go to the hospital. When we met her, she had no money, and without a place to crash, she was headed to Tennessee to stay with her aunt and uncle. She repeated throughout our conversation, "It's just a bad situation. A really bad situation."

We tried to encourage Amber as best we could. We didn't want her to feel weird or uncomfortable. We just wanted to love on and help her in any way we could. She said a number of times, "Oh my gosh. You guys are so nice. Why are you doing all this for me?" Funny, we weren't doing much but giving her something to eat and spending time with her.

While we talked, we were approached multiple times by people wanting a picture or autograph. Curious about the attention, Amber asked what I did.

"I run a foundation," I said.

Eyebrows raised, she turned to Anne and asked, "What kind of foundation is that?"

The three of us were the first ones to board our flight. It was neat being able to give Amber this experience, especially since she was so nervous traveling by herself. Anne and I settled Amber in her seat before getting in our

own. Even though we were sitting apart from her, we didn't want Amber to feel like she was stranded. Before takeoff, Anne spent a little more time with her, talking to and praying with her. She gave her some literature that shared the gospel message. Finally, Anne assured Amber we would help escort her to her next flight.

After we touched down in Atlanta, a Delta agent led the three of us off the plane. Before pointing out where she needed to go, we prayed with her. I gave her the cash I had in my wallet and promised we'd keep in touch. Since the time of writing this book, it's been a little over a year since I met Amber. And I've heard more of her story.

Amber's mom had died recently at quite a young age. Her sudden death rocked Amber's world. As a result of this trauma and her abusive relationship with that past boyfriend, Amber suffered from depression, anxiety, and PTSD. Finding herself homeless was a breaking point.

> When we try to put ourselves in other people's shoes, we can give them hope.

Right before the trip to Tennessee, Amber remembers sleeping on a bench at night and sobbing, "I can't do this anymore. I just can't." She'd run out of money. Her friends who had lent her money were broke themselves. Unable to find a shelter that had vacancy, Amber was desperate. She contemplated punching a police officer so she could get arrested and spend a night or two in jail. Hey, it meant sleeping somewhere warm. The next day, out of the blue, Amber got a call from her aunt, her mother's sister. And this was the current situation when we met her. This aunt asked if Amber wanted to stay with her in Tennessee for a while. It was an answer to prayer.

Since that time, Amber has moved back to New Jersey. A lot has happened since then. She is in the process of going back to school and trying to rekindle her artwork, one of her creative passions. She has found a place to live. She is also engaged.

At the time of writing this chapter, I spoke at an event in New Jersey that I had invited Amber to attend. I ended my talk that day by giving people there the opportunity to trust Jesus. I was so excited to learn Amber accepted the invitation to receive this free gift. This young lady has overcome so much in her life. Amber told me, "So many people in my life thought I was a failure. They said I'd never amount to anything. But I'm a survivor. I'm not exactly where I want to be, but I'm working on getting better. There is a light at the end of the tunnel."

When we try to put ourselves in other people's shoes, we can give them hope. We can give them a brighter day. We can help make a difference in their lives. Today, Amber has more hope and peace in her heart than she's ever had. That's awesome!

WHAT DO YOU SEE?

Though I try real hard to stay in the moment and notice the world and the people around me, it's easy to get distracted. This happened right after I finished my first season of baseball. I finally had the time to catch up with different projects and book some speaking events, but I found myself so focused on everything I had to do that I wasn't able to pay attention to life unfolding around me.

I remember being on a plane after speaking somewhere and being convicted of this. I wrote down, "I want to have open eyes to people's needs, not wanting eyes to my needs." I wanted to get better at putting myself and my needs aside. I still don't do it right all the time, but I try my best.

Why is this hard for any of us to do?

We live in a world of distractions. We are always busy with something. Our schedules are packed. Our minds spin with endless responsibilities. It seems we are always rushing here and there, juggling several things at once in the name of trying to multitask and be efficient. This can blind us to life—the life we're living and the life happening around us.

I think about being in the airport when I met Amber. With Christmas fast approaching, travel plans increasing, gift lists growing, and lines getting longer, thousands of passengers hustled at a seemingly manic pace trying to go here or get there—and fast. But this kind of behavior is not just evident around the holidays. I travel often, so I'm at airports a few times a week. I see this all the time!

People rush around, not caring about the others they bump into, cut in front of, or say something short to. It's like most people are so eager to get to their destinations that they forget about everyone else around them. Now, it's okay to look forward to where you want to go. It's okay to get excited about a flight that's on time. And it's okay to be efficient and multitask. But somewhere in the middle of all this, you can lose sight of the importance of paying attention to others.

I've found in my life that one of the best places to minister to people is in airports. Here's what I mean: I already know everyone I work with, everyone in my family, and everyone on my team. But the minute I step into an airport, I come face to face with hundreds of strangers. Strangers who may be struggling through a rough time. Strangers who may need a hand. Strangers who may secretly long for a kind word.

Awareness is a lost art. While this comes naturally to some people, it's a trait that any of us can learn. Playing sports all my life and being the youngest of five siblings have taught me about spatial awareness: being attentive to my surroundings, anticipating moves, reading people. This has crossed over from the field to my personal life. Though over the years I've become more aware of what happens around me, I'm still a work in progress.

I'll admit, there are times I walk into an airport and I can't wait to get on the plane, slink into my seat, put on my headphones, and watch a good movie. And there is nothing wrong with that. At the same time, we can all benefit from not just focusing on the end goal but also paying mind to the space around us. There might be an opportunity to make a difference. And who doesn't want to do that? You could be paying for your coffee and notice someone a few feet away who's been crying. Take a minute and ask if there is something you can do.

Look, it's not about being perfect. And it's not about putting everything in your life on hold so you can help or talk to or encourage every single person who crosses your path. It's just about keeping things in perspective. It's about slowing down and opening your eyes enough to see others. To see a world that exists outside your own. To see people who need help. To see people who are hurting.

I promise you this: if you open your eyes to actually see people, you'll begin to uniquely see certain people. I'm more attuned to people who have special needs. You may be moved toward noticing people who struggle with depression. Make this your mission. Be intentional in broadening your spatial awareness. Ask God to take the blinders of distraction off your eyes and show you people who may need you. Then use the opportunity to help them out, lift up their spirits, or guide them where they need to go.

WHAT GOD SEES

Let's take this a step further. Sometimes opening our eyes means seeing others on a deeper level than what's being presented on the surface. Since

I've been talking about traveling, picture with me this scene at an airport. You're standing in line, waiting to check in your bag, and you notice a man at the counter in front of you going ballistic. Say the airline overbooked his flight and he was just told he had to give up his seat. You watch as he waves his hands all around and yells at the agent in frustration. You might think something like, *Oh man, what a jerk.*

Now, this man may be acting like a jerk, but consider looking at this situation from a different angle. Either you can determine in your mind that he is simply behaving badly, or you can consider that maybe, just maybe, he has been out of town for a week, misses his kids so much, and all day he has been anticipating getting to see them in a few hours. And then he is told, "Sorry, but that's not going to happen." It's easier to feel more sympathy for someone in this scenario, isn't it? Maybe he's not such a jerk after all. Maybe he's just a devoted dad who simply wants to go home and be with his family.

It's interesting what happens when we cast a situation, or a person, in a different light. I think we see others better when we humanize them or consider, even without knowing for sure, something they may be going through or struggling with that causes them to act a certain way.

There's something about seeing people as particular individuals, not as a whole. In this, we get a more personal picture. This is how God views us human beings. He considers us individually—and He loves us individually.

I was visiting a prison in Florida at the time I was working on this chapter. Being there reminded me how important it is to see each person as an individual, as someone God values so much that He sent His Son to die for that person. This is true of every single individual on this planet.

Over the years, I've met a wide variety of inmates. Some are hardened and have no interest in talking. Others smile a lot and can chat with you for hours. Some look like they could hardly hurt a fly. Others act like they want to hurt everyone around them. And God loves each and every one of them . . . the same.

While sometimes, in unique situations, I'm told why the inmates I'm talking to are in prison, I typically don't want to know. It can be blinding. It can make it somewhat difficult to share with them about love, grace, and hope. Seems it's much easier to identify these people by their crimes and maybe not want to minister to them.

But this is not how God sees them. And this is not how God sees us. We've all sinned. We've all fallen short of His glory. But no matter how bad, illegal, corrupt, or evil the things we've done, He doesn't call us by our sin. God calls each and every one of us by name. I'm so grateful God doesn't look at me and see my failures and my mistakes. And I want to honor Him by viewing others His way.

Whenever I visit a prison, the needs are great and the lack of hope alarming. I've met with hundreds of men on death row, scheduled to die in weeks or even days. I've seen men on suicide watch, just waiting for an opportunity to end their own lives.

On one visit, I remember this man who was one of the most pleasant and respectful inmates I had ever talked to. Even the correction officers agreed this man treated everyone around him cordially. This one time, I saw him in the yard. I shook his hand through a fence and we talked for a little bit. He told me about his brother being a huge Gator fan and thanked me for visiting.

As I walked away, one of the officers asked me, "Do you want to know what he did?"

I wasn't so sure.

The officer proceeded to tell a detailed story of how this inmate had raped and killed a little girl many years ago. His crime was despicable. Utter evil. As disgusted as I was listening to what this man had done, and as much as I wanted to throw up in that moment, the fact is God still loves him. In fact, God loves this man just as much, no more and no less, than God loves you and me. And if this man who committed such an abominable act against an innocent child was the only person on the planet, Jesus still would have loved him enough to die for him.

It's crazy to think about, isn't it? I can't understand or fathom the depth of God's love. But one thing I know is that we must live by our convictions, not by our emotions. Human feelings won't always allow us to have grace, love, or mercy for another human being who may not, in our own eyes, deserve it. But viewing others through a God lens will.

I remember in the same prison visit praying with a group of inmates. These were hardened men who had committed serious crimes. One of them had seen me around the prison a few times over the years. He said, "Man, you really do love us, don't you, Tim?"

I nodded and replied, "I do. I really do."

"But how?" he asked.

"Because God loves you."

Loving others is not optional. As followers of Jesus, we don't get to love certain people and not others. Jesus said, "So now I am giving you a new commandment: Love each other. Just as I have loved you, you should love each other" (John 13:34). As hard as it may be to love certain people, it's much easier to do when we ask God to help us see them the way He does.

A New Lens

I remember meeting a young Hispanic girl in a wheelchair during a meet and greet at an event. Let me first say that because our foundation has a big heart for people with special needs, I'm always around kids or young adults who have disabilities. To me, they are special. They are loved. And no matter how badly they hurt, inside or outside, God has a special plan for them. I know this, but there are moments, and I don't even know how to begin to describe this, when I will meet someone with special needs and feel what I can only explain as a hint of the depth of God's love for us.

It happened when I walked up to this girl. She was beautiful to me. I wished the world could see the beauty that I saw in her face. I gave her a hug. In that moment, it seemed like she was the only person in that room. This is so hard to put into words, but I felt like I saw her as more than just a girl. She was love. Though we had never met before, she knew I loved her and I knew she loved me. It was a love that can be ascribed only to God, our heavenly Father, who sees us, knows us, and loves us beyond our comprehension.

Now, I don't get this feeling around everybody. I'll admit that just as I see people as special and loved, sometimes I see people as a burden or a distraction. Like the obnoxious guys who shove their way toward me to have me sign something I know they are going to sell on eBay for a quick buck. But every now and then, I believe God opens my eyes to see others the way He sees them. And the more this happens, the more desperate I am to look at people through a lens that is not my own. I want to see people the way God sees them, the way a mother looks at her baby or a hopeless romantic looks at his significant other.

How do you see people? How do you want to see them?

As believers, we need to see people not as the world sees them, not even as we, in our frail human minds, see them. We need to see a different picture. The world may look at someone with special needs and see her as less than. The world may look at someone who is hurting and pretend he is not even there. The world may look at an addict and see her as hopeless. The world may look at someone struggling with many problems and see him as baggage. But it's not just the world that does this. We all do.

Sometimes we judge people based on what we see on the outside. A man in a fancy Italian suit walks by, and we may see him as successful. We meet a beautiful woman with a seemingly perfect husband and two seemingly perfect kids, and we may assume she has it all together.

Whether we look at people and see them based on their successes or failures, their triumphs or mistakes, God does not. We need to make the choice to try and see what God sees and try to love as God does. It's really hard to love everyone, and always, if we try and do it on our own.

I remember hanging out with my brother Robby while I was training for baseball. One night, a friend of ours had rented out space at a bowling alley and invited us to hang with some of his friends. Now, I'm not a championship bowler, but I'm always game for doing something fun.

When we pulled into the back of the building, I remember seeing a few homeless people. I didn't stop, but I didn't forget them either.

Not long after we settled in, my friend's crew joined us. This group happened to include a handful of pretty girls. All of a sudden, the room got a little bit brighter. We broke into two teams. It didn't take long for some to start the smack talk. Even the ones who couldn't bowl to save their lives had something sharp to say. We all had a great time poking fun at those who rolled slow gutter balls and cheering when someone on our team scored a strike.

As the evening died down, and after chatting it up with the one girl who caught my eye, everyone headed out the back to wait for their Uber rides. It was late. It was dark. I wanted to make sure everyone got home okay. We milled around. Still talking. Still laughing. Me still getting to know the one girl I found intriguing. As much fun as I was still having, I couldn't escape this thought that pressed on my mind: *You saw them earlier. They're not far away.*

Without streetlights, I couldn't see more than a few feet in front of me. But as I turned to my right, from the corner of my eye, I noticed a few homeless people on the sidewalk. They seemed to melt into the shadows. Ragged and dirty, some clutched tattered blankets, others plastic bags filled with their most precious, or only, belongings. A few huddled up together, eating something out of a torn-up carton that looked like it had come from a trash can.

> I want to see
> what God sees.

My eyes fell on this one man closest to me, about thirty feet away. He was in a wheelchair and looked to be dozing on and off. Something about him moved me. I could see his army fatigues sticking out from under his military issue blanket. I wondered if he was a vet. Maybe he had served our country.

It's easy to look at someone who is begging for some change and see a person wanting the next high or a drink or two or a pack of smokes. I don't want to think this way. I want to be the kind of man who looks at another human being and sees a soul. I don't want to judge someone by my assumptions or by that person's actions. I want to see what God sees.

Not wanting to draw attention to myself, I quietly crept away from the crew and walked toward this man. As I approached him, he was looking at me from the corner of his half-closed eyes. "Hi, sir," I said.

No response.

I coughed and said a little louder this time, "Hi there."

He nodded and opened his eyes a bit wider.

I handed him some money and said, "I just wanted to give you this. God bless you." The man looked at me for a few seconds, confused. Then he simply nodded in acknowledgment. And that was that.

He stayed on the streets, and I walked back to my friends.

I'm not sharing this to make you feel guilty about not stopping at every homeless person you see or to get you to start giving every homeless person you see some cash. I want to invite you, in the middle of busyness or even in the middle of fun and laughter and chatting it up with a potential coffee date, to stop. Remember that in the midst of whatever you are doing, people around you are hurting. And if you ask God to open your eyes in whatever you are doing, He can show you an opportunity to impact someone's life, whether in a big or a small way. It can come at any time, at any place, in the middle of anything you do. You just need to be ready for it.

And stop and *see.*

MAKE THIS YOUR DAY

As believers, we often talk about being the hands and feet of Jesus, but why does this act of service stop the minute we step into an airport terminal? Or the grocery store? Or at the hotel pool on vacation? Or any place we find ourselves outside our daily routine?

We live in a society that is focused on social media or phones or whatever gadget is in our pocket or hand. It's like anytime we have a second to sit down—whether it's in an airport, at the dinner table, in class, or at work—we bury our heads in our devices. Emailing. Texting. Scrolling. Browsing. We're so enveloped in this veil of distraction that we've forgotten what it's like to stop.

To open our eyes.

To be part of life.

To look around.

To notice people.

To smile.

To say hello.

To see a need . . . and fill it.

Stop for a second and embrace the now. Take a breath and focus on what's around you. See if there is a place where you can make a positive impact. What can you do? If the answer is obvious, do it.

9

THIS IS THE DAY
Live with Open Hands

We make a living by what we get. We make a life by what we give.

—Anonymous

Some of us live like we have control over the rest of our lives. And with closed fists, we grip tightly to our resources, time, talents, skills, and money. We think we have all the time in the world to do what we want and how we want it. We think that one day we'll pay attention to how and when God nudges us. We convince ourselves that one day we'll do what really matters. But living with a tight grip is not really living at all. It's living under the false illusion that we have control.

———

The second I stepped into the prison infirmary, I locked eyes with an inmate covered in tattoos. And I mean covered. Even every inch of his shaved head sported ink. John was flanked by two armed guards. They never took their eyes off him the entire time I was there.

John sat at a table. A nurse in front of him Velcroed shut a padded vinyl cuff around one of his upper arms. With both wrists shackled together, his hands rested in his lap, arms pinned to his sides. I noticed a long metal chain that stretched from the steel handcuffs on his wrists to one securing both of his ankles. It rattled every time he moved.

"How are you doin', man?" I asked, slapping him on the chest.

John's eyes grew wide. "Whoa! Hey! It's Tim Tebow!"

The nurse squeezed the balloon mechanism to inflate the cuff around his arm.

"They testing your blood pressure?" I asked, reaching my hand out toward his. "You doing all right?"

John laughed. "Yeah, I'm fine, man." Jerking his head toward one of the officers towering over him, he said, "They be trying to tell me I stabbed someone today."

Never a dull moment in prison.

"Well, that's not good. You can't be going around stabbing people," I said.

"You right, man," John quipped with a smirk. "You right."

I dropped on a knee right beside him. I wanted to get close to him, maintaining eye level. It was a way to show him we were equal. I wasn't there to judge him. I was there to show him I cared. More importantly, that God loved him.

John told me he was from a small town in Florida and was a huge Gator fan. We chatted about football, debating who our school's next coach would be. Then he talked about his mother.

After a few minutes I asked, "So how can I pray for you today, John?"

Silence. He shifted in his seat, the chains rattling. "Well," he began, "you can pray for my mom. She's going through a tough time right now. She needs the prayers more than I do."

"You got it. What's her name?"

After he told me, I said, "Okay, I'll pray for your mom. But what about you? How can I pray for you?" I hated repeating myself. I wasn't trying to be annoying. I just wanted to dig a little deeper. I wondered what was going through John's heart in that moment.

I stared straight into his eyes. As he squirmed in his seat, they brimmed with tears. Maybe he wrestled with guilt. Maybe he was haunted by something he'd done. Maybe he doubted his self-worth. Maybe he didn't believe he could ever be forgiven.

"Just pray for my mom, dude. I got a lot on my mind."

"Sure thing," I said. "But I don't want to leave without telling you something. John, I want you to know that God loves you. He has a plan for you. I know you're chained in cuffs right now. I can't even imagine how hard that must be. But God loves you. Matter of fact, He loves you so much that He gave His only Son, Jesus, for you. See, John, Jesus took your place on a cross and died for you. God loves you so much, and He wants you to know Him and have a close relationship with Him."

John nodded slowly. Fighting back the tears, he shifted his eyes away from mine. The jangle of chains echoed in the room.

We talked a bit more, mainly about his mother. Before I left, still crouched by the table, I said, "I just have one question before I go. John, would you like to put your faith in Jesus today? Would you ask Him to forgive you for your past and begin today to have a personal relationship with Him?"

I knew his heart was saying yes, but his pride was telling him no. Which voice was he going to listen to?

John shook his head. "No, man. Like I said, I just got a lot on my mind."
I had to ask one more time. "Are you sure?"

"Yeah, yeah, yeah. Maybe I will one day." John smiled, then said, "And if I do, I'm going to be thinking of you, Tim."

"Well, I hope you do, John. I want you to have the peace of knowing Jesus. He desperately loves you. And He wants you to know Him."

I got off my knee and put a hand on John's shoulder. "I'll be praying for you and your mom," I said.

John looked down at the table, the metal on his cuffs gleaming under the ceiling lights. Long seconds passed in silence before he looked up and said, "Thanks, man."

I walked out of the infirmary that day, my heart heavy. Whispering a prayer for John and his mother, I couldn't stop thinking about this man. I could tell something about our conversation had moved him. Something was bothering him; he was under conviction. He was uncomfortable for a reason.

God was working on him, but John fought it. He fought the stirring in his soul. He fought the chance to trust Jesus. He fought for control over his emotions, his life, and ultimately his destiny. He thought this was something he could consider one day, tomorrow, but he wasn't promised another day. None of us are.

THE ILLUSION OF CONTROL

How often do we fight for control? Over our lives, our money, our time, our stuff? How often do we fight to trust Jesus when storms come? How often do we fight to give Him our future? How often do we fight doing the right thing?

The reality is that we can't control everything. So many of us worry and live in fear, trying to make things happen or not happen. But we can't control the uncontrollable. We can't stop the unstoppable. Who knows what tomorrow will bring? I don't. You don't either.

We can focus only on today. Right now. This moment.

When we live this way, our grip loosens. Our fingers uncurl. Our hearts begin to open. We live with open minds and open spirits, willing to step out in faith and allow God to take us where He wants us to go and do things He wants us to do.

Money is a great example of the challenge many people have of living with open hands. People want money. They want more than what they have. They want more than what their neighbors have.
Some hoard it. Others spend it. Some use it wisely. Others use it foolishly.

Now, money is not a bad thing. We all need it. We can't pay our rent, our mortgages, or our electric bills if we don't have any. The Bible tells us,

> The reality is that we can't control everything.

"For the love of money is the root of all kinds of evil. And some people, craving money, have wandered from the true faith and pierced themselves with many sorrows" (1 Timothy 6:10).

Many people get this verse confused. Money isn't the problem. The *love of* money is. Money becomes problematic when you fall in love with it, when you let it control your decisions, your impulses, and your actions.

My dad modeled how to live with open hands when it comes to finances. We didn't have much growing up, but we never lacked for anything. For instance, we couldn't afford to go on family vacations for a time, but God would always provide. Someone would call my parents and offer a vacation home somewhere for us to use. Things like that happened all the time.

My parents were generous with what they had. I talked about this in chapter 3. They trusted God so much with what little they had, they often gave it away to help someone else. I'm so grateful my parents taught me how to live with open hands. Having accumulated some money over the years, I know well the temptation to buy stuff for the sake of having it instead of staying focused on what really matters.

I remember as a little boy flying on airplanes at night. It was such a big deal. I'd look out the window and marvel at the blanket of lights stretching as far as my eyes could see. *What a big world,* I'd think. Now whenever I'm traveling, I have a different perspective. I still see a big world. I also see a hurting one.

My platform opens many doors to talk to different people all over the world. I often see two extremes in one day. One morning I'll be in Washington, DC, for the National Prayer Breakfast, and at night I'll be speaking to inmates on death row. The disparity between the haves and the have-nots is real. This perspective is truly sobering. And saddening. It reminds me how so many people are lost. How so many people need to be encouraged. How so many people need hope. How so many people need the love of Jesus.

Living with open hands gives us a chance to make a difference. We may not be able to change the entire world, but we each can change the world of at least one person. God gives us certain talents, abilities, resources, and even money. We don't have these things so we can try and impress others but so that we can impact those around us for good. You might not think what you have is much, but God will use whatever that is in ways you can't imagine.

THE IN-BETWEEN

Sometimes in the course of wanting to live differently and make an impact on others, we miss the mark. I'm reminded of something that happened while I was writing this book.

LIVE WITH OPEN HANDS

I find God often nudges my heart to notice certain people and situations. I try my best to do what I feel He is leading me to do, but I don't always get it right. But even when I try to excuse away His promptings, I find if I admit I didn't pay attention and remain willing to be used, God will do some pretty amazing things. I've learned that even when we're not at our best, God is always at His best.

My fever had been raging for two straight days. And along with feeling like I was gulping razor blades every time I talked or swallowed, I couldn't wait to hop on the plane and rest during the flight. I'd found out that morning I had strep throat. Seriously? I thought that was something only little kids got!

I walked with Anne toward the gate, a baseball cap perched low over my face, my headphones on. Most of the time when I travel, I try to stay under the radar. When approached, I don't mind talking to folks who recognize me and taking a photo or two. But today I felt so lousy I just wanted to get on that plane and watch a movie. It was not to be . . .

Suddenly, I noticed a man with a cane walking in front of me. He had a pronounced limp. Every time he stepped on his right foot, his leg would bend unusually far to the right. I wanted to say something to him. I didn't know exactly what, but my heart was moved to talk to the guy.

I tried to figure out in my head what to say. Everything I could think of just sounded weird. "Hey, I noticed you were limping and, uh, how can I pray for you?" I don't know about you, but for me, as friendly as I try to be and as much as I enjoy connecting with people, sometimes it feels uncomfortable to approach a stranger out of the blue. It's easy to talk to someone if you have a reason to. But going up to a guy with a bum leg without an excuse didn't seem like the greatest idea in the world. Talk about awkward!

Another thing. As I watched him, there were travelers galore who were pointing and staring at me, whispering to whomever they were with, "Is that Tim Tebow?" Stopping this man in the middle of a busy terminal would invite a scene. That seemed a reasonable excuse to keep walking.

But that pull to talk to the man with the cane remained.

Then, from the corner of my eye, I saw a shop that sold my favorite sparkling water. Whenever I'm at this airport, which is pretty often, I have a ritual of buying my drinks here. I stared at the back of this man's head. As he continued walking forward, I peeled off to the right to get my sparkling water. Instead of following what I felt God nudging me to do, I stuck with my routine. As I paid for the beverages, the guilt pressed in on me. I told Anne what had happened and said, "Let's go find him."

We took off into the terminal, determined to find a needle in a haystack. We shot glances around every gate. We peeked into every store. Nothing. I never saw this man again.

With only a few minutes left before our flight was scheduled to board, I sat down across from my gate. *Timmy,* I thought, *you're an idiot!* I remember writing down, "Sometimes in order to make an impact, you have to put yourself in an uncomfortable position."

Living with open hands doesn't always mean the opportunities that present themselves will come with perfect timing or feel totally natural. In fact, I've found it's usually the opposite. Think about it. How many times has someone tapped you on the shoulder and said, "Hi. Can you tell me about Jesus? I really want to know Him." Or, "I feel so lost. How can I find peace?" Sometimes we must take the risk that people will be initially annoyed or weirded out by our striking up a conversation for the ultimate purpose of encouraging them.

Feeling stung by disappointment made me feel worse on top of being sick. So I prayed silently, *God, I know I missed that chance. But please, give me one more.* As I uttered the last word in my mind, eyes glued to the ground, I glanced to the right. My eyes stumbled across two prosthetic legs. I looked up and saw a man in his late twenties walking by. He carried a military backpack, slapped with an American flag sticker. On one of his legs flashed another flag. My adrenaline started rushing. I had asked God to give me a chance to brighten someone's day, and in the next second, I saw someone whose body was literally broken.

As I jumped out of my seat to the right to introduce myself, two flight attendants on my left bounced toward me to ask for a picture. *Nooooo!* I couldn't ramble off with the speed of an auctioneer to these two women, "Sorry I gotta run I can't take a picture with you I missed an opportunity I felt God giving me and I just got another one and I really can't miss it this time so sorry not sorry but I have to run. Bye."

"Grab that guy," I blurted to Anne just before agreeing to take the picture.

"What guy?" she asked.

"The one with no legs," I exclaimed, pointing to the man I'd just seen.

She dashed away as I smiled for the camera, all the while thinking about the opportunity that was just put in front of me. When I saw Anne and this young man walking toward me three minutes later, I felt relieved. I still didn't know what I was going to say to him exactly. I was just so excited to actually have the chance.

"Hi, I'm Tim," I said, holding out my hand to shake his. "It's so nice to meet you. I just wanted to thank you for your service."

The young man introduced himself as David. In our brief conversation, I learned he was stationed for a few years in Afghanistan. Halfway through his deployment, he walked into a building and unknowingly stepped on a bomb. Upon impact, this young man shot up in the air. Both of his legs were

THIS IS THE DAY

blown off, as well as half of one arm. For six months, doctors deemed him a triple amputee, but miraculously they were ultimately able to salvage his arm. They could not, however, save his legs.

We took a picture together and talked more before an airline employee announced our flight was boarding. While Anne hustled to board, I hung back at the gate, toward the side of the multiple boarding lanes. I don't know exactly why I waited—maybe I was hoping for a last chance to see the man with the cane. *Hey, you never know.*

As I watched the mass of passengers line up in their respective lanes, a few people came up to me. One guy told me his sister was a runner at *SEC Nation.* As I talked to him and his wife, a woman approached with tears in her eyes.

"Thank you for what you did for the Lato family," she said. My heart fell. She was talking about Alexis Lato, a teenage girl who had recently passed away from neurofibromatosis. I first met Alexis in 2012, when our foundation granted her a W15H. You'll read her story in the last chapter.

Alexis was an incredible example of living life to the fullest. Her motto was YODO, "You only die once." Despite the sixteen tumors that slowly destroyed her body, her attitude was amazing. Contagious. She brought so much light wherever she went. She often talked about coming back as an angel. My angel. "Timmy, just so you know, when I get to heaven, I'm going to be with you in the outfield. When you make a diving catch, I'll be your angel and help you get it done." I don't think I did near as much for the Lato family as this woman said. Alexis did plenty more for me and, I'm sure, for every single person she met.

As I was talking to this woman who knew the Lato family, I noticed David line up in one of the boarding lanes. I had no idea he was on our flight. Suddenly, I felt these arms wrap around me in a bear hug. It was a buddy of mine, Billy Horschel, a pro golfer I went to college with. It was great to see him. Billy had just withdrawn from a tournament because of a shoulder injury, so I tried to encourage him. Billy and I boarded the plane together. As I plopped down next to Anne, settling in with my iPad and my headphones, my heart felt uneasy. I turned to her and said, "I really think I need to offer David my seat."

"He can take mine," Anne offered graciously.

"Thanks, but no. I'd like to give him my seat. I just want him to know how much I appreciate him."

I waited until most of the passengers were seated, then started walking down the aisle into the coach section. I tapped one of the flight attendants on the shoulder and said, "Ma'am, I don't want to make a big deal out of this, but there is a man sitting a few rows back. He has two prosthetic legs. Would you please ask him if he would mind switching seats with me in first class?"

She looked at me and said, "Of course. I know exactly who you are talking about," and hurried down the aisle toward the back of the plane.

When this flight attendant came back, she shook her head. "He said he's fine where he is, but thank you."

I wasn't ready to give up. "No, seriously. Would you mind, please, going back there and talking to him again? Tell him I really, really want him to."

A minute or two passed, and finally, I saw David walking toward me. "Thanks, man," he said with a grin. "You didn't have to do this." I clapped him on the shoulder and said, "I just appreciate you and everything you've done for this country." I meant every word.

Long story short, the flight attendant directed me toward another empty seat. I sat down and started pulling out my iPad and headphones. My throat burned. I was starting to sweat. The fever was back. A few people around started saying hello, but I was ready to watch a good movie. And rest.

That didn't happen.

The minute I sat down in the aisle seat, trying to figure out a comfortable position, I thought, *Man, what did I do? They don't make plane seats for people who power squat!* As we took off, the two ladies seated in my row started talking to me. They told me they were from Denver. Yeah, I could see where this conversation was going.

These two ladies, who happened to be super sweet and really cool, had a knack for questions. Most women do. I know this—I have two sisters. These fellow passengers asked me about the foundation. I was happy to share some things with them. Then, just as I grabbed my headphones, they asked about baseball. I talked some, fiddling with the wires. I had a feeling I wouldn't be watching the movie. Then they showed me pictures of their kids. I enjoyed their company, but at that point, my throat was on fire. By the time one of them had asked what it was like growing up in the Philippines, I finally accepted the fact I would not be watching the movie.

Ten minutes before landing, one of the women showed me a cool picture. I couldn't tell at first, but it was taken from the ground, pointing up at these beautiful buildings. The way the light hit the detailed etchings and curves of the structure made it appear as if there were a shadow, or an outline, of a cross in the background. This woman explained how the picture meant something to her. Then she mentioned something about divine intervention, how maybe it meant something that I had sat down next to her.

She cleared her throat, trying to choke back emotion. I noticed tears in her eyes. "Maybe God is trying to tell me something," she said almost in a whisper.

"What would He be trying to tell you?" I asked softly.

The woman looked down at her hands. She started rubbing her wedding ring as tears slipped down her cheeks. The plane landed with a thud on the runway. I can't remember exactly what I said, but I tried my best to encourage her. Then I gave this woman my email address and offered to pray for her. Hundreds of seat belts unclicked on the plane, and passengers rushed to remove their bags from the overhead bins. The three of us stood up, ready to disembark. I gave them both hugs as we exchanged long goodbyes.

I went to look for Anne, all the while thinking I hadn't done enough for this woman who had been visibly upset. Turned out, Anne had left something on the plane, so I asked her to meet me by baggage claim.

When I got to the carousel, I noticed the same woman I had been talking to on the plane near the rental car counter. I had an idea. Instead of just telling her I would pray for her, I could do better. I jogged up to her and said, "Hey, I mentioned I'd be praying for you, but if you'd be okay with it, maybe we can pray together right now."

Holding back tears, she said, "Sure, that would be great."

We ambled over to an area on the side that was relatively quiet and had a few empty rows of seats. With our eyes closed, I prayed that God would use whatever she was going through for good. I prayed for a wall of protection around her life. I prayed that even if others had betrayed her, God would remind her that He would never let her down. Afterward, she shared pieces of her story. A struggling marriage. Two kids. Trying to make it work but not feeling hopeful. She shed a few tears before we said our final goodbye.

We might not be able to fix what people are going through, but we can be a part of their journey. No one should have to experience the hard stuff in life alone. We can pray with each other. We can listen to each other. We can walk alongside each other.

It's so easy to get caught up in life and ignore or say no to situations where, as uncomfortable as they may seem at first, we can make an impact. Even after I acted like an idiot and didn't walk up to the man with the cane, when I was finally willing to be open and not miss another opportunity, God stepped up. He always does.

Don't wait to be the hands and feet of Jesus only when you sign up for a mission trip or volunteer for a local service project. Be ready to give in the in-between. Sometimes these can end up being the biggest moments in our lives.

MAKE THIS YOUR DAY

You don't know what can happen when you follow God's prompting. You never know who needs your help, who needs your encouragement, who needs your love, who needs the message of hope Jesus came to this world to bring. It's not all about us, of course. It's about being a vehicle through which God can work in the lives of others.

When you're not feeling well, when you're going through a battle of your own, or when the last thing you want to do is talk to another person, be open. Be ready to give. This is the day to open your hands.

When is the last time you truly lived with open hands, when you opened your heart or gave of your resources, time, talents, or finances? What did you learn from that experience? How would your life look if you lived this way every day?

10

THIS IS THE DAY

Flip the Script

Have I not commanded you? Be strong
and courageous. Do not be afraid; do
not be discouraged, for the LORD your
God will be with you wherever you go.

—Joshua 1:9, NIV

R ecently I had an interesting conversation with a few television producers
in my field. They all happened to be single. We got on the topic of significant others, the pros and cons of not having one, and the quest to find one.
The conversation got pretty deep quickly.

One said, "I'm too busy to commit to dating seriously." Another re-
marked how "dating is just too much trouble." One person even mentioned
something about how having a significant other would hinder his career.
Another admitted to being on the verge of giving up on finding someone
special because she felt so frustrated by the process.

I appreciated these men and women being open and sharing their different perspectives. And I could certainly relate to the point about being busy. I
know what it's like to have a hectic schedule and juggle many responsibilities.
Dating someone seriously with those kinds of variables can be tricky for sure.

In my opinion, however, it's just not a big enough reason to not try. And that's where I wanted to offer some encouragement. We should never lose hope, especially as it concerns relationships. And I'm not just talking about significant others.

I believe we are made to be in relationships. With God first, then with others. For me, others include my family, my friends, and hopefully one day a significant other. Community is truly what life is about. I believe investing in relationships is worth far more than any career choice I could make.

Now, I'm not saying we single people should throw ourselves into the dating pool with reckless abandon. Nor should we open our hearts to just anyone simply because we'd prefer not to be alone. I just believe if we have a desire to be married one day, it's important to stay open and trust God through this process.

WHAT IF?

If you're single and dating or single and wanting to date, I know the questions that accompany the journey. Things like:

What if she's not the one?

What if he breaks my heart?

What if she says no?

What if he turns out to be a psycho?

What if this is just a waste of my time?

What if I keep dating and dating and dating and I never find "the one"?

What if?

What if?

What if?

This is a question that lingers in most of our minds, not just as it concerns dating but with life in general. What if my child gets sick? What if marriage counseling won't help? What if I don't get that job? What if I do?

Sometimes our fears of the what-ifs are legitimate. Other times they are totally irrational. Either way, when we obsess over this question in any area, it can cripple us. And it becomes impossible for us to live a full life.

It comes down to this simple but powerful truth: God is bigger than our questions. When we trust Him in every decision we make, we can be confident knowing that "God causes everything to work together for the good of those who love God and are called according to His purpose" (Romans 8:28). And even if a

> God is bigger than our questions.

situation doesn't work out as we hoped it would—whether a relationship, a career, or a dream—we can still learn and grow from it. And when we give the experience to Him, God will somehow in His own way use it for good.

This reminds me of a story. Tune in because I don't write or talk about this often. And it might be one that you can relate to.

During an off-season in football, I had been talking to this young lady. She was sweet, loved Jesus, and was very easy on the eyes. I had planned a day trip with some of my close friends and family at this incredible resort. We loved getting up to the mountains whenever we could. This was the perfect opportunity to spend time with her and my closest and trusted friends in a gorgeous setting.

We all met up for breakfast first. There were plenty of laughs, great conversations, and definitely a lot of chemistry between this young lady and me. I noticed she was wearing a cool shirt. It showed a little skin, a patch of a shoulder, to be exact. She wore it well, and I told her so. But I liked more than just her style. The more we talked, the more I learned we had much in common. Or so it would appear. Whenever I told her I liked this band or that movie or this book or that idea, she'd chime in with an excited "Me too!" It was like this all day.

Deciding to take off to the snow after breakfast, some of our crew wanted to hit the slopes with their skis or snowboards, but others, me included, opted to snowmobile. I'd already broken my leg once in high school. I didn't want to see that happen again.

We agreed to meet up at the front of the lodge. My friend Bryan, his wife, Tina, and I waited for this girl to show up. Bundled up in heavy coats and ridiculous layers of clothing, we were ready to fight the freeze aboard these fast snow machines.

Five minutes passed. Then ten. Then fifteen. She still hadn't shown up. I was starting to worry, but then I got a text from her saying she was just getting ready and would be down in a minute. Having two older sisters, I know how important the "getting ready" ritual is, especially if there is a date involved. Now, I love me a girl who takes care of herself. But, truth is, I don't get excited about it when it takes a long time. Like a real long time. And, side note, definitely not when within that long time a face is rubbed, dabbed, powdered, and dusted with so much makeup, I can't even see skin. I'm a natural beauty kind of man. Trust me on this, ladies. You don't need so much stuff on your face!

Finally, the front door to the lodge opened and out she popped. I noticed she had changed her shirt. It was the same exact style as the one I had complimented her on earlier that morning. That was cool, kinda, but it was freezing outside. I mean, part of my eyebrows were starting to turn into icicles.

I didn't want this girl to get frostbite. So, after giving her a hug, I asked, "Are you sure you're not going to be cold?"

"Nope," she replied with a smile. "I'm okay."

"Seriously, we can wait if you want to get a jacket or something," Tina suggested.

She shook her head. She was fine wearing just that. I thought it odd, but, hey, maybe she loved handling herself in bone-crushing chill. And maybe I had just found the one thing we didn't have in common. But whether she wanted to or not, there was no way I was going to let her freeze. I ran into the lodge and hunted down a parka for her to wear.

Finally, we were all ready to brave the cold. We hopped on our snowmobiles and raced off through a winter wonderland landscape. As we wove through aspen trees frosted with ice and snow, the scenery was breathtaking. Snowmobiling was awesome, but with the icy powder blasting our faces, this young lady and I didn't get much of a chance to talk. When we got back to the lodge for some well-earned hot chocolate, we had more conversations.

Getting to know more about her over the next few hours made me think one of two things. Either the girl was the total package or she was putting on a front. My gut was starting to question the stream of "me toos." In her defense, early dates can be somewhat nerve racking. I know I always want to make a great impression on the person I'm with. But good impressions aside, it's important to be yourself. Sharing things in common is awesome, but differences in tastes or opinions are fine too. Hey, life would be boring if we were all the same.

Some of my friends picked up on this too. Bryan and Tina, who are always looking out for me, mentioned something about wanting to get to know this girl more. I remember at dinner, as I chewed a bite of steak, I heard Tina ask this young lady, "So, tell me about your family." I tuned in immediately. I was curious where Tina would drive this conversation. By the time I had demolished my steak, I hadn't learned anything more about her. She just seemed more comfortable with "me too"–type answers.

The same crew met up the following weekend at my house for dinner. I walked into the kitchen and noticed a cheese platter someone had laid out. I don't know about you, but I'm not a fan of fancy cheeses. To me, they look anything but appetizing. I don't know which one it was, but I remember staring at either moldy blue cheese or a cube that looked like it had just come out of someone's dirty toes. I almost threw up in my mouth.

"Ugh," I said, gagging. "That is absolutely disgusting. That cheese looks like it's three thousand years old!"

"I know!" this girl piped up. "I would never eat that."

I found out later that she had told someone in our group that she loved cheese. In fact, she made this statement while happily gobbling up one of the moldy cubes.

After that incident, I wasn't super interested. It wasn't about the cheese. I don't care if a person likes cheese or not. It was disappointing that this girl felt she couldn't be herself and say what she really meant. I want to find the real in people, not the perfect, because the perfect does not exist. Hey, I have my own quirks and habits. There are things I like and things I don't. Not everyone agrees with me on everything—and that's okay!

> You don't have to change who you are to fit the ideal of another person.

If marriage is your goal, I pray you find the right person. Just know you can be honest and open about who you are. You don't have to put on a facade. As much as I enjoy dressing up and looking nice, at the end of the day, I don't want a woman to fall in love with how I present myself. I want her to fall in love with my heart, real and all.

You don't have to change who you are to fit the ideal of another person.

And if it's not enough for him or her, that's okay. Remember, you are enough because God created you in His image and for a unique purpose and plan.

In any case, relationships are tough! Whether you're dating, going through a divorce, or trying to work through a strained friendship, these are not easy roads to navigate. Sometimes it seems easier to just give up on people or to shut down emotionally ourselves. But this is just fear talking. And God is bigger than our greatest fears.

I haven't handled every relationship well. There have been friendships where I wish I could have done better or said something more useful or even kept my mouth shut, but I'm encouraged that God can use even my mistakes. And this gives me hope. I don't have to approach future relationships with fear, questioning, or doubt. I can rest in His providence. I can be confident He's got my back.

A Different Way of Thinking

Taking a chance or even doing the right thing doesn't always equal a fairy-tale ending. But just because something doesn't work out doesn't mean we failed or that our pursuit of that passion, dream, idea, or challenge was pointless.

Are you willing to risk for what may turn out to be incredible, life changing, or meaningful? Or for the potential of creating a new chapter in your life that may be scary at first but just might be the greatest adventure of your entire life?

I think of my pursuit of baseball and the negative criticism the media and others have drawn from it. *It's a joke. He's a joke. He has zero chance to make it.* Etcetera, etcetera, etcetera.

Well, so what if I don't make it? At least I can say with confidence that I gave it my all. I don't know about you, but I don't think there's much of a downside there. So instead of focusing on the fact that some people have already destined me for failure and others fear I'll embarrass myself, I'd prefer to wonder, *What if I do make it? What if that something I love so much and am fighting so hard for does work out? What if I actually get to the majors as a thirty-year-old man who hadn't played in over ten years?* Wow! Can you imagine?

My life, my passions, my dreams, my ideas, my plans, and my goals are not defined by the potential pitfalls, by what others say will happen, or by worst-case scenarios. I can't even imagine living this way. It must be awful! That's not living at all.

Look, I have days when it seems everything goes wrong. In these times, I pray and try to see the best in every situation. It's not that I ignore the obvious. I just try and choose to not let fear take over my decisions or my actions. I try and determine to see the positives in people and circumstances that are not the greatest. I try and trust God over my doubts. Do you see how much trying I do? I don't get it right every time. This is something I strive to do. It's about taking slow steps, little steps, each day to make better choices.

I know so many people who hate their jobs. Most of them tell me they would rather stay where they are, hating every minute of it, just because they fear losing financial security or letting their families down. These are legitimate concerns.

> Nothing is perfect. Not people, not stuff, not positions.

We can't all live our dream jobs in every stage of our lives. And frankly, I don't even know if a dream job exists. Nothing is perfect. Not people, not stuff, not positions. Living out a dream you have achieved comes with hard work and sacrifices, even when it seems you've gotten what you wanted. What's most important is living a life of purpose, meaning, and significance—something that's possible even if you're not thrilled with what happens between the hours you clock in and clock out.

In whatever you do, there must be some sort of payoff. There needs to be a reason why you sit behind a desk for eight hours or change diapers all day long or teach math to middle school students five days a week. I believe the significance comes in two ways—and both revolve around relationships. See, everything always comes back to people.

One, you can find meaning if you have a positive influence over the environment where you work. And two, you can find purpose through the money you make (things like securing your family's future by saving or paying off debt, investing in a mission trip, or helping those in need).

In our culture, money can change lives. The point is not to work to make money for the sake of accumulating wealth. The point is to use that financial resource to make a difference in the life of your family or in others' lives. If neither one of these things is going to happen in your current job, it might be time to consider a new plan.

Most of us need to work. I don't know anyone who can afford to lounge around all day while the bills are being magically paid by a fairy somewhere. It's important not just to have a job or a career but to have impact somehow through these things. My goal is not to have a career. When I'm lying on my deathbed, taking my last breath, I don't want someone to hold my hand and say, "Timmy, you had one heck of a career." I would rather someone say, "Timmy, you really had a huge impact on people!"

Please don't think I'm telling you to quit your job right now and expect another to come knocking on your door tomorrow. It's about trusting God and finding meaning in whatever you do, wherever you are.

It's also about knowing that even when life is tough, like when you don't have the option to do everything you want or your calculated plans go awry, you can choose not to let these hardships destroy you. You can choose to trust God, even when your present circumstances feel overwhelming or even hopeless.

BIGGER THAN THE GIANTS

I think about Sarah Borders. In 2009 this eight-year-old girl was diagnosed with Ewing sarcoma. For the next seven years, Sarah fought against this giant of cancer. She battled with more than just the physical weapons of chemotherapy, radiation, and multiple surgeries; she also fought with resilience, grace, and courage.

It's never easy to fight the giants that stand before us. But life is full of them, isn't it? There are giants of the unknown, giants of fear, giants of doubt, giants of insecurity. Some of these giants get in the way of our living and enjoying life. They keep us up at night. They taunt us day after day. They tell us that we're not good enough, that we'll never make it, that we might as well stop trying and give up.

Here's the good news: God is bigger than any giant we may face. This is a truth that Sarah chose to believe. Instead of focusing on how powerful the giant of cancer was, Sarah knew that God is bigger and more powerful than a deadly disease. Talk about flipping the script! Instead of letting fear overwhelm her, she was confident in her faith. Instead of cowering in anxiety, she chose to fight. Instead of giving up, Sarah chose to hope.

In the beginning of 2016, the disease progressed to the point that doctors could no longer treat it. They had no hope to offer. Outside of giving her an oxygen tank so she could breathe and meds to make her comfortable, there was nothing they could do. Sarah was put on hospice, but this girl was a fighter. And as her mom, Missy, put it, "She still had a lot of living left to do."

Sarah wasn't ready to give up. There was something she really wanted to do before it was time for her to go home to Jesus. Sarah was looking forward to attending a Night to Shine prom. She wanted to dance. She wanted to feel beautiful. She wanted to feel like a princess. Even if it was for one last time. She asked a special friend, Matthew, to be her date to this prom.

So Sarah gritted her teeth and fought with everything she had. She told her mom every day, "I have to go to the Night to Shine prom. I just have to!" On Monday, February 8, 2016, a day after her sixteenth birthday and four days before Night to Shine, Sarah took a turn for the worse. The hospice nurse estimated she had six to eight hours left to live. She gently suggested to Missy that family and friends come over to say goodbye.

Sarah slept the rest of the day. She slept all day Tuesday. By Wednesday, she was still sleeping. Then, a miracle. On Thursday evening, the day before Night to Shine, Sarah woke up. "I'm going downstairs," she announced. "I have to get ready for prom." Sarah's family was in shock. They couldn't believe what they were seeing and hearing.

This was the same girl who was given a death sentence. The same girl who had been sleeping for the past three days. The same girl who was too weak to leave her bed for the last two weeks. Imagine the shock when Sarah, helped by a family member and her pastor, walked downstairs and then sat in her wheelchair for forty-five minutes. Missy believes this was Sarah's "trial run" for Night to Shine.

The morning of the prom, Sarah woke up with a pep in her step. "Mama, we've got to hurry. I've got to get ready."

Missy was thrilled, yet cautious. "Honey, are you sure this is a good idea?"

"Yes, Mama. Let's go. I need to get my nails done."

So Sarah began to prepare for Night to Shine. She got a manicure and pedicure with a friend. A nurse's daughter, who happened to be a makeup artist and in town that day, came over and offered her cosmetic services. As Sarah rested on her bed, she was beautified—hair, makeup, the works. Afterward, Missy and her mother helped Sarah slip into her favorite dress. It was bright pink, adorned with sparkles and layers of delicate ruffles. Then, the final touch. Sarah placed a pink glittery hat on top of her bald head. She was all smiles, glowing. Her mom wasn't sure her daughter would be well enough to stay at the prom the entire time, but she hoped for the best. This was Sarah's night.

When Sarah and Matthew pulled up to the red carpet at a church in Cedartown, Georgia, Sarah refused to be helped out of the car by the volunteers who hustled toward it when it arrived. She wanted Matthew to do it. It was their first date, after all. Sarah beamed while Matthew rolled her down the red carpet as a crowd of people lining the sides clapped and cheered.

The first thing on Sarah's mind the minute she entered the decked-out ballroom was chocolate. "Take me to the fondue station, please," she told Matthew. Sarah hadn't eaten in the last four days, but that night she was going to have her fill of chocolate. Later, she headed to the karaoke room and belted out Martina McBride's "This One's for the Girls." From the corner of the ballroom, with tears in her eyes, Missy watched her daughter sing. Then, Sarah danced. Oh, did she dance. And not just in her wheelchair. This radiant princess stood up and on her own two feet twirled in her beautiful pink dress all over that dance floor.

On the ride home, happy but exhausted, Sarah whispered to her grandmother, "Dadgey, this was the best night of my life. This is a dream come true. I know I'm living on borrowed time, but this was worth everything." Before she drifted off to sleep that night, Sarah told her mom, "I'm not scared of dying, Mama. I know who Jesus is."

The next morning, Sarah's house was filled with family, friends, and people from church and the local community. They'd all heard about this miracle. Forming a prayer and praise chain, they stood in a long line that stretched from right outside her door down to the first floor and out the front door down the driveway. One of her friends asked Sarah what she wanted to do the next day. Sarah looked at her and smiled. "I won't be here tomorrow. I had a dream and I saw Jesus's face. You might think I'm crazy, but I'm going home tomorrow on Valentine's Day."

The next day, February 14, she asked her mom to invite different people into her room. She first called for her brother, Richard, and her grandmother. She loved on them. They loved on her. Then Sarah made a list of people to whom she wanted to give little gifts. A few hours passed. She was getting more and more tired. Before the night was over, on that Valentine's Day, Sarah went home to be with Jesus. I have a feeling she's dancing with Him right now.

To Sarah, cancer was never bigger than her God. Through her story, so many people came to know Jesus. So many people got encouraged. So many people found hope. I have been so inspired by Sarah. She has reminded me that no matter how hard the battles we face against things like cancer, depression, divorce, fear, or loneliness, our God is always bigger. And we must choose to believe it, no matter what our circumstances dictate.

> Our world is full of hurting people who just want someone to come alongside them.

As impossible as it may seem sometimes, we can fight the giants in front of us because we know that we are not alone. God is with us. He is before us. He is behind us. He is right by our side. We may have to face some uncomfortable times. We might have to face some really hard times.

But we don't have to do it on our own because the God of this universe is always with us.

What a powerful truth to live by! This should give you strength to trade your fears, your doubts, and your questions for hope. And this should move you to help someone else do the same.

Many people today are fighting for their lives. Our world is full of hurting people who just want someone to come alongside them and help them face whatever giants stand in their way. They long for someone to say, "I love you. I believe in you. And despite what your circumstances look like right now, God has a special plan for your life." God wants us to look around, find someone, and say:

"If this means holding a prom for you and buying you a beautiful pink dress, I'll do it."

"If this means preparing a meal for you, I'll do it."

"If this means helping you clean up your house, I'll do it."

"If this means chopping down a tree for you, I'll do it."

"If this means cheering for you, I'll do it."

"If this means bringing you to church, I'll do it."

"If this means praying for you, I'll do it."

"If this means watching your kids for you, I'll do it."

"If this means holding your hand, I'll do it."

"If this means giving you a hug, I'll do it."

"If this means reminding you that you matter, I'll do it."

"If this means not giving up on you, I'll do it."

When we stand with God and with others and fight the good fight of faith instead of fearing the unknown, we will not be defeated. The giants before us will fall.

MAKE THIS YOUR DAY

How often do we allow fear of the what-ifs to keep us from simply trying? Why do we often imagine worst-case scenarios? And why do so many of us allow these fears to keep us from reaching for something or from following a desire we believe God has put on our hearts? What if instead of thinking about what-ifs in a negative light, we use them to imagine the positives?

- What if I make it?
- What if I find that special someone?
- What if this open door leads to somewhere amazing?
- What if I succeed?
- What if my idea actually works?
- What if I *can* make a difference?

Think about your life. Do you give yourself a chance for your greatest potential to shine through? Or is the battle lost before it's even fought? Instead of letting the negative what-ifs to paralyze you, choose to allow the positive what-ifs to give you hope for the future. Flip the script.

In whatever situation you are in, what can you do right now to begin to believe you can overcome in the midst of fear instead of doubting or giving up?

11

Go Back to the Well

God is the only source of hope that'll never disappoint. When we place our faith in him, he provides joy, peace, and hope that overflows.

—Rick Warren

At one point while playing for the Denver Broncos, I remember being the focus of endless chatter. A stream of negative and positive opinions were thrown at me from every direction. I couldn't get away from it. I passed billboards that celebrated me and while going incognito overheard conversations criticizing me.

I remember driving home one night, bombarded by these voices. I decided to watch a couple of highlight reels. I had to remind myself of my potential. I had to remind myself of the wins. Most of all, I had to remind myself that God created me in His image and that He had a plan for my life.

As an athlete, confidence is key. And it's something you can't lose. I had to be confident no matter what people would say. And for me, that meant going back to the well—remembering who I am in Christ!

KNOW YOUR TITLE

A few weeks after Hurricane Irma hit, I was preparing for a talk I was scheduled to give at a certain event. I couldn't stop thinking about how many Christians struggle with insecurity. Many feel inadequate, not good enough, not talented enough, not skilled enough. Many believe they don't have much to offer in the way of making a difference.

I remembered what it was like traveling with Governor Scott, Senator Rubio, and the major general. These were super-powerful people. They command respect simply because of their positions. It was interesting to watch these men walk into a room. People would stop talking to one another. They would put their phones away. They would straighten up and pay attention. Wherever these men go and whatever they do, they have confidence knowing that—beyond their experience and knowledge, of course—their titles give them power.

I wondered how many believers live each day with as much confidence and assurance as powerful men and women who hold impressive titles. Maybe you do. Maybe you don't. We all should.

As followers of Jesus, we are called God's children (see John 1:12). We are sons and daughters of the Creator of the universe, the King of kings, the Lord of lords. That's pretty amazing—and pretty impressive! As I prepared for my talk, I wrote down my title: child of God, son of the King of the world who will forever reign.

Who are you? A child of God? A son? A daughter?

Know your title. And never forget it. When you don't feel you are enough, understand that you can conquer self-doubt by knowing who you are in Jesus. This is truth. And this is life changing, not just for you, but for others.

Here's the thing about your title as a child of God: The title is for your benefit! You don't need it acknowledged by others. Your title gives you the confidence to live each day with faith. It gives you the courage to tackle whatever giant towers over you.

Our title reminds us who has our back. It reminds us that even when we walk through the valley of the shadow of death, we don't have to fear evil because God is with us (see Psalm 23:4). Going through dark times sucks. We may lose a battle, but we have good news. God has won the war.

Living out that confidence through your title, however, ultimately is for the benefit of others. People don't care about your title. It doesn't matter to them. What's important is what you can do for others because of your position. Because of your title, you can be armed with courage to do hard things, to share with others the good news, to help those who need it. This is what matters.

Knowing who we are can help us make the right choices that can make a difference in the lives of other people.

LOOK BACK AND REMEMBER

Going back to the well is important to do, not just in sports but in life. Our faith in what God says about us transcends everything we do, on and off the field. So when we're feeling down or tired or unmotivated, we can trust that God has us where we are for a reason, even when things aren't going great.

Let's be real. Most of us don't wake up every day feeling "on" or thinking life is just fabulous. I don't. It's hard to be at your peak all the time and have incredible determination and discipline and make every right decision each and every day. Some days feel like an uphill climb. Sometimes you get sick. Sometimes your kids get sick. Sometimes you don't sleep well. Sometimes you feel empty or worn out. Sometimes in the process of trying to reach a goal or make a difference, you might lose that passionate feeling. Sometimes you feel bummed out because someone said something hurtful.

Any number of things can happen that put our emotions into a tailspin. This is why going back to the well, our Source, is important.

> Any number of things can happen that put our emotions into a tailspin.

When we've lost our motivation, we need to look back and remember what created our motivation in the first place. This is a spiritual practice. Instead of reminding yourself of your own highlight reels, like your accomplishments, your successes, or the awesome things others have said about you, there's a better way to reignite your momentum.

When you're just not feeling it, remember when you first trusted Jesus. Remember the moment when you were convicted in your spirit and overwhelmed by His grace. Remember the moment when you believed with your whole heart that God has a plan for you. Remember the moment you learned that your life was not an accident and that you have a unique purpose. Remember the time you shared the hope of the good news with a friend who made the decision to trust Jesus. Remember the song you sang in church or at a concert that so enraptured you in God's presence, you could almost feel Him.

Look back and remember.

Know that God is consistent. He was faithful then and He'll continue to be. Now, this doesn't mean He will always give us everything we ask for or answer every prayer in the way we want. Still, God is the same yesterday, today, and forever. Second Timothy 2:13 tells us, "If we are unfaithful, he remains faithful, for he cannot deny who he is." Being faithful is who God is. It's His nature. It's His character. You can count on this!

Looking back and remembering is not about living in the past. It's not about focusing on the "good old days." It's about using our past experiences to drive us forward. It's about remembering that even in our failures, even on our bad days, even when we don't feel like we deserve it, God can redeem it all.

There's always hope. God is always working behind the scenes. When we remind ourselves of this truth, it can help us stay grounded, no matter what we're going through.

It's Not About Us

On October 28, 2012, I was a backup quarterback for the New York Jets. (Yeah, that didn't go so well.) In that game, we were getting crushed by the Miami Dolphins. By halftime we were down 20–0. While I was on the field, I kept thinking, *Okay, this is going to be my chance. We're getting blown out, but any minute now they're going to put me in. They have to! And when they do, I'm going to have another come-from-behind victory, just like in Denver, and I'm going to turn this thing around.* But the Dolphins continued to roll past our team, tacking on another touchdown. *Any minute now, any minute.* The opportunity never came. We lost big, 30–9.

It was a tough game for us, especially because we had been on a losing streak. I hate losing. I'm sure you know this by now. In the locker room, the mood was foul. Nobody smiled. Nobody talked much. Maybe the only good thing happening was that this was our bye week—no game next Sunday.

Suddenly, a team of security guys rushed into the room and rallied us together for an announcement. "Folks, we've got ourselves an emergency. Three storms are colliding right now and creating the perfect storm. Her name is Hurricane Sandy. You don't have much time to waste. So whatever you're going to do, do it now. If you're planning on getting out of town, leave now. If you plan on staying, hunker down immediately. This is going to be a big one."

Some of my friends and family were at the game, so I dashed out of the locker room to get together with them and figure out our plans. We decided to try and get home to Florida. Hurricane Sandy threatened to shut down New York City and surrounding areas for days. Airports all over the Northeast were starting to cancel and ground flights. Thankfully, we managed to hop on a plane that would take us home.

It didn't take long after takeoff for us to fly right into beating rain. Gusty winds rushed sideways. The plane bobbed in the air like a rag doll from the unrelenting turbulence. Our seat belts were buckled so tight they pressed into our clothing. You can believe everyone on that plane was praying.

I can't remember how long it was, but eventually the murky clouds parted, slowly revealing clear blue sky. When we finally touched down in Jacksonville, Florida, some clapped while others breathed sighs of relief.

As grateful as I was that we had made it home safely, I wrestled with deep disappointment. I had missed my opportunity to change the game. To me, on that day, I was still the most important thing.

At the same time, over eight thousand miles away in the Philippines, a nineteen-month-old little girl named Jocy was getting hungry for breakfast. As the toddler's belly rumbled, Judith, Jocy's mom, began preparing the meal. Judith quickly realized she had run out of water. She picked up an empty bucket and ran to the well, leaving Jocy at home with her sister, Kajiah, three.

Small brooms made of natural fibers are common in the Philippines. While used for cleaning the house, they can create a fire hazard. Unfortunately, Kajiah, being a curious toddler, innocently lit the broom on fire.

As Judith filled her bucket with water from the well, from the corner of her eye, she saw smoke rising. Squinting in the light of day, she realized it was coming from her house. Judith dropped the bucket of water and raced back. When she arrived, bright orange flames licked the walls of her house. Heart racing, she ran to the window, saw her two daughters, and with great courage pulled them out to safety.

In shock, Judith hugged her girls tightly as their home turned into a great pile of ashes on the ground. They lost everything in the fire, but Judith was grateful her two girls survived. As the shock wore off, this mother took a breath and looked over her girls to see if they had sustained any injuries. Kajiah escaped with minor burns. When Judith inspected Jocy, however, her heart fell. Jocy's skin was starting to melt off her arms and her back, layer after layer after layer.

Judith rushed with her girls to the hospital. Emergency room doctors started to remove more layers of Jocy's skin. While the burns were severe and required extensive treatment, early skin grafting for one, doctors didn't do much more than apply ointment to her wounds and bandage them up. She was discharged after two weeks with just a prescription.

Without the proper and critical treatment Jocy needed, her wounds did not heal. Her burned skin contracted, leaving her arms and hands severely deformed. Over time, the contractions got worse. Six months after the accident, her forearms and fingers were fused to her upper arms like little wings. Because of the severity of her injuries, Jocy's quality of life drastically diminished. She couldn't feed, bathe, or dress herself. She couldn't play with her dolls. She couldn't climb a tree. She couldn't even go to school. Jocy relied on her parents to do everything for her.

For the next three years, Jocy went to clinic after clinic. All who examined this precious girl were baffled by her condition and had no idea how to fix her. She saw specialist after specialist. Their only solution, which wasn't even a guarantee, demanded hundreds of thousands of dollars in surgery and therapy. Her family couldn't afford a penny of it. They could barely get by as it was.

Jocy was heartbroken. Her parents tried their best to keep her hopes up. They told her over and over, "One day, you're going to be better . . . One day, you're going to use your arms . . . One day, you're going to feed yourself . . . One day, you're going to ride a bike." Jocy's mom prayed every day that God would somehow provide a way for her daughter to get the right treatment and live a normal life.

When Jocy was four years old, her parents called a charity organization in their village and asked if they could help their daughter. "I'm sorry, we don't have the resources," they were told.

Then, a miracle. More than a year later, this organization remembered Jocy. A new hospital had opened in Davao City, about three hours away. Maybe they could do something. This was the Tebow CURE Hospital. Jocy and her family were overwhelmed with hope. Doctors at our hospital were willing to take on this little girl's condition and see what they could do. One of our CUREkids coordinators said this about Jocy when she arrived: "A lot of kids come in scared and meek and timid. . . . Jocy walked in, and while she wasn't super chatty or outgoing, there was this fierceness to her. She came in with a warrior spirit. We were rooting for her since day one."

After a doctor examined five-year-old Jocy, he thought for a moment, then said, "Let's pray about this and put together a plan." Jocy's first surgery was scheduled on June 14, which happens to be my brother Peter's birthday. While it was a success, Jocy's injuries were so complex, she required more surgeries and months of physical therapy. Six months later, Jocy sat on an examination table in the hospital, her parents by her side. It was her last appointment. This was the final unveiling. A doctor uncurled the last of the bandages on Jocy's little arms. Then he took her arms in his hands and stretched them all the way up and then out, parallel to the ground. With tears in his eyes, he said, "It's a miracle. I really didn't think this was possible. This is truly a miracle!"

Today, Jocy has full mobility in her upper body. She doesn't have to rely on her parents to do everything for her. She can feed herself. She can bathe herself. She can brush her teeth. She can catch and throw a ball. She can even ride a bike. When Jocy was in the hospital, her family told her she could have anything she wanted at the end of all her surgeries. Jocy didn't have to think twice. "A pink bike with a basket," she said. We all worked together to make sure she got her wish.

> "Let's pray about this and put together a plan."

While Jocy's physical body was repaired, she also discovered newfound freedom. It's evident in her confidence, her smile, her laugh. After one of the hospital coordinators spent some time with this little girl teaching her how to ride her new bike, Jocy was determined to do it on her own. Clutching the handlebars while trying to steady her balance, she declared, "Just give me little pushes. I can do it."

When I was making it all about me after that Jets game, a little girl on the other side of the world was about to get her world turned upside down. At the exact same time I was flying out of a storm, Jocy was walking into one. I think about not just how I initially lost perspective in this situation but how God was working behind the scenes. At the same time I was feeling bummed about not being a starting quarterback, our foundation decided to build a hospital in the Philippines, the same one that would help Jocy get her life back after being told there was no hope for her.

It's not always about us. But without consistently going back to the well and remembering what's most important, this can be a hard principle to live out. Each day tugs us in different directions. It's easy to lose perspective. It's easy to get lost. It's easy to get wrapped up in whatever we're trying to do or whatever we're struggling with. Without consistently reminding ourselves of what God says is most important, we'll stumble around, void of purpose, never leaving a mark on this world. Each day requires us to go back to the well. That's where we find truth. That's where we find comfort. That's where we find hope. That's where we will always be reminded that as believers in Jesus, we serve a God who is always working behind the scenes, all over the world.

MAKE THIS YOUR DAY

What does the phrase "go back to the well" mean for you? More important, how do you do it? How do you go back to the well? For me, it's about recharging my soul with God. This is not a complicated process, yet it's full of meaning and purpose. Sometimes I read one of my favorite Bible verses and reflect on God's truth. Sometimes I play a moving worship song. Sometimes I remind myself of a sermon that provoked, challenged, or inspired me in some way.

Going back to the well looks different for everyone. The point is to connect with God, knowing you are His child. Remember your title. Spend time with Him in prayer. Read His Word. Thank Him for bringing you through tough times. Thank Him for His provision. Thank Him for His faithfulness. Try writing down your testimony. This can be a powerful experience.

One more thing: When I'm feeling drained and need to be

motivated by Jesus, one of the ways I go back to the well is by serving others. I visit a local hospital and spend time with kids in need. This helps keep my perspective in the right place. This is also an example of how God's economy works. When we give of ourselves, we are built up. On the other hand, when we constantly take from others, we become empty.

If you feel your spiritual life is a bit stale, what's something different you can do to connect with God?

12

THIS IS THE DAY

Make It Count

Do you know that nothing you do in this life will ever matter, unless it is about loving God and loving the people He has made?

—Francis Chan

YODO! You only die once!" Sixteen-year-old Alexis burst out with a grin after handing her mother a copy of her bucket list.

Elise looked at the piece of paper marked with writing.

Swim with the dolphins. *Okay, we can do that.*

Celebrate all holidays. *Christmas in July sounds fun.*

Toilet paper someone's house. *What?*

Get a tattoo. *Alexis! A tattoo? Are you serious?* Elise's eyes bulged out of her head.

Alexis shrugged her shoulders and smiled even wider. She always smiled, even throughout her battle with neurofibromatosis (NF2). One day when she was twelve, Alexis felt unusually dizzy and started suffering from double vision. After multiple tests and MRIs, doctors found twelve tumors inside her body and diagnosed the rare genetic disease. Over the next four years, these tumors would grow and mutate, compromising Alexis's ability to walk, hear, see, and ultimately breathe.

YODO was Alexis's motto. Elise had never heard of such a thing. To her, at first it sounded morbid. To her daughter, however, it was a reminder to enjoy life, to seize the moment, and to check things off her bucket list, no matter how bad she felt or how sick she was. YODO meant even more than this.

Elise told me, "Since Alexis first started saying YODO, it's been in my head. She taught me not just to live life to the fullest or like today is my last day but to also *love* life to its fullest. Love life when it is great. Love life when it is hard. And love life when it is just okay. I have learned to love life even more than living life."

Wow, this is a girl who knows how to make life count.

I met Alexis in 2012 through our foundation's W15H program. We were blessed to host her at the Jets versus Cardinals game in New York. Even from the moment I first saw her, her passionate enthusiasm and energetic spirit were evident. In a wheelchair and suffering from partial vision and hearing loss, Alexis was also full of life. She gained strength from God, knowing He was always with her, knowing He loved her, and knowing that even in her darkest times, He had a special plan and a purpose for her life. I like to think this is why Alexis never stopped smiling. Her father, Patrick, said, "My daughter saw life in a way that has taught us more than we ever taught her."

> She never viewed her sister as a burden, but as a best friend.

Alexis was truly one of the greatest examples I know of someone who lived to the fullest. No matter how sick she was, she refused to lie around and do nothing. She wanted to enjoy her family, her friends. She wanted to be part of something. Alexis was determined to create special moments. Many of these were made with her sister, Emma, two years younger. Emma was a rock to Alexis, always showing great strength. She never viewed her sister as a burden, but as a best friend. The two were inseparable and spent countless nights together in the living room. Whenever Alexis would sleep there, Emma would move the couch right up to her bed so the two of them could hold hands and watch movies. The bond these two shared was indescribable, and a testament to great love.

When Alexis was first diagnosed with NF2, doctors wouldn't allow her to play sports because of her double vision. An avid softball and volleyball player, she didn't want to just sit out and give up playing. So Alexis asked her volleyball coach if she could manage the team. Of course he said yes. Even after her first stroke, she remained committed to the job.

This attitude resonated in everything Alexis did. When she was homebound or in the hospital, she continued her studies, maintaining straight As. Alexis pursued wholeheartedly what she loved—school and sports—without excuse and without even considering what others viewed as limitations or setbacks.

As unfair and unexplainable as her physical condition seemed, Alexis knew that whatever the reason, this was the path laid out for her. And she determined to walk it with strength, dignity, and passion. It was her way. The only way.

Elise told me, "Alexis never let NF2 be who she was. When I look back at our journey and what she went through, Alexis thought of her disease almost as a gift. She would just tell us that God has given her a special plan. She not only saw this; she used this plan."

Alexis didn't just do things she wanted to do; she also had a heart filled with compassion for others. She sent birthday cards celebrating friends. She wrote letters of encouragement to those who needed hope. She lifted the spirits of others who were sick.

Elise remembers one time visiting a hospital in Maryland for treatment and on the way back stopping at Georgetown Cupcake. "Alexis just loved some of those cupcakes," Elise told me. "As we left the shop, our daughter noticed a homeless man near the door. But she didn't mention anything at that point. We got in the car, and as soon as I started chowing down on my mouth-watering cupcake, Alexis said, 'Wait, I want to give that man my cupcake.' I was shocked. She only had one cupcake for herself. I offered her mine, but Alexis refused to take it. 'It's not about that,' she told me. 'I just want to give my cupcake to him.' That was Alexis for you, always thinking of others."

Her selflessness showed in the way people rallied around her. Her volleyball team sponsored an Alexis Lato night. They decorated the gymnasium in her favorite colors and sold T-shirts they had made, inscribed with the words "Fight like Lato." In an emotional ceremony, the team retired her jersey that night, number 10. When Alexis was a freshman and admitted to an inpatient rehabilitation facility, the senior members of her school's softball team opted to forgo hanging out at the much-anticipated county fair to spend hours with Alexis. She had a blast playing Ping-Pong and silly games with these girls.

I remember sometime in the middle of May 2017 talking to Alexis after one of her doctors had given her some bad news. Already having endured multiple strokes and the complications of all those tumors attacking her body, one which pressed dangerously on her spine, she learned her prognosis was grim. Alexis had the option to undergo clinical trial treatments. She refused. She was firm in her decision and told her parents, "This is how I want to finish my life," then added, "I hope you're not mad."

Less than two months later, I was blessed to have Alexis visit with me in Port St. Lucie while I was playing with the Mets. I spent a few hours with her and her sweet parents before the game. I brought in a few of my teammates to join us so they could have the pleasure of meeting this amazing young lady. Though Alexis had suffered total hearing loss at that point, we communicated with her through a speech-to-text app on her phone. We talked. We laughed. We prayed. Our time together was full of hugs and joyful moments. I felt so blessed to have Alexis be a part of our family for almost five years. She was truly a special girl. One of the last things I told her was, "I'm so proud of you, Alexis. You are changing so many lives. I love you." And she said to me, with a wide smile, "I'm gonna be your angel in the outfield, Timmy. You just watch."

On September 24, 2017, Alexis was lying in bed in her hospice room, listening to music. This girl loved to sing. In fact, when she became deaf, it didn't stop her from belting out songs to her favorite musicals. I imagine it was the sweetest voice to all who heard her. As Alexis's body began to shut down that day, the song "For Good" from the Broadway hit *Wicked* was playing in the background. Elise sang along softly as her daughter's eyes closed. Then Alexis took her last breath. She was finally home, in the arms of Jesus.

The last line of the song sums up this amazing girl and her impact on everyone she met: "Because I knew you, I have been changed for good."

Alexis crossed off much of her bucket list. Though she didn't get to toilet paper a friend's house, she did celebrate all holidays (including Christmas in July and Halloween in August). She swam with dolphins. She even got sworn in by the local police department as an officer. And yes, Alexis got her tattoo. She chose the Hawaiian word *ohana*, a running theme of the Disney movie *Lilo & Stitch*. It means "family. Family means nobody gets left behind or forgotten."

Since Alexis went home to be with Jesus and inspired a mass of people to live each day to the fullest, some of her loved ones have gotten *ohana* tattoos. Her cousins, a few friends, both of her godparents, a hospice nurse, and her parents each sport ink that will forever remind them of this beautiful young lady.

Alexis will never be forgotten.

MAKE A MOMENT

I've talked throughout this book about how we must choose to live in the moment, this day. I've also shared a lot about purpose and passion. Perhaps as you've been reading these pages, your heart has been charged. Maybe a new dream has surfaced. Maybe an old one has been reignited. Maybe you've made a goal to be more intentional with your time. Maybe you've decided that this is the day to do something that truly matters.

In the first chapter I talked about how important it is for me to create meaningful moments. This might sound scripted on some level. It's anything but. Think about the physical body. If we're sick, outside of a miracle performed by God, we cannot necessarily heal ourselves. We may not be able to keep ourselves from getting sick, but what we can do is create an environment where our bodies can thrive. We can eat the right foods. We can take the right supplements. We can put ourselves in a position physically where we have the most potential to be well.

This same principle translates into life. Though we don't know what tomorrow holds, nor do we have the power to manipulate life in our favor all the time, we can be intentional with finding significance.

Here's one way to do this: Think about a time in your life when you truly felt the most in line with your purpose. Maybe it was when you started mentoring a teenager in your community. Maybe it was when you led a Bible study for the first time. Maybe it was when you encouraged a single mom. Maybe it was when you served in a soup kitchen. Maybe it was when you went on your first mission trip. It could be any number of things, but remember the feelings you had. Peace. Joy. Love. Contentment. Passion. You might even say it felt like being home.

> For Christians,
> the world is
> not our home.

I have many moments like these, but one of the most special is during Night to Shine. Within a little over a twenty-four-hour period, I'm on a plane bouncing from country to country all over the world, from Africa to Haiti, and in cities across the United States to attend these proms. I meet thousands of people with special needs, some who maybe for the first time in their lives feel special and loved and are treated like royalty. At the end of the night, after each guest is crowned prom king or prom queen, my hope is that every single one leaves a decked-out ballroom knowing that God loves each of them and has a special, unique, and purposeful plan for his or her life. When it's time for me to head home, usually around three or four in the morning, by that point I haven't slept for forty-eight hours. I've been fueled by pure adrenaline. I love every minute of it. Every. Single. Minute. My soul is on fire. This, to me, feels like home.

For Christians, the world is not our home. Ultimately, we belong with God in His heavenly kingdom. This place on earth is temporary. I do believe we get glimpses of our home with God when we are aligned with His promises and purpose for our lives. When we are living for Jesus, when we are serving Him with our God-given gifts, talents, and abilities, when we are investing in people, when we are thinking of others more than ourselves, when we are changing lives, one at a time, we get a sense of our true home in God.

I want to challenge you to put yourself in places where you feel that sense of home, places where you are consumed with purpose and significance. This doesn't mean following a script or reenacting exact moments. That should take some pressure off! It means stepping out in faith and allowing God to do the rest. It means being willing to let Him use you. It means making the time to encourage someone else. It also means looking for opportunities to rise to the occasion and taking them when they come.

Make People Count

I've said often that life is about people, relationships. Saying "I love you" is one thing, but doing something for someone is perhaps the greatest way to show that person matters.

I love buying gifts for people. I especially love buying extravagant gifts for those closest to me. Now, I'm a frugal person in general, but when it matters most I'm not so much—like when it comes to supporting causes I believe in or buying something for my parents or my siblings.

There's something powerful to me about watching loved ones open presents. I get a kick out of seeing the look of surprise and gratitude on their faces. It's priceless. Over the years, my family and I have become huge fans of jewelry designer David Yurman. And having the opportunity to meet him a few times and attend several of his events has been pretty cool! Not to mention the fact that his company donates a portion of the price of some of my purchases to our foundation.

One year I gave my two sisters and my mom rings by David Yurman. They came from his one-of-a-kind collection. Masterfully crafted with precious metals and crowned with rare gemstones, only five of these unique pieces were created.

I remember one Christmas a few years ago thinking about what I could give my mom. While browsing in one of David Yurman's showrooms, I started talking with one of the managers. He shared with me about this exquisite bracelet they fly around the country to showcase at different boutiques and events. It was a one-of-one piece. I asked to see it. He pulled out this beautiful piece of jewelry, drowning in brilliant diamonds. Against a backdrop of black velvet, the bracelet dazzled. No doubt about it, it was gorgeous. It was also ridiculously expensive. But I couldn't help but think about Mom.

On one hand, it cost a stupid amount of money. On the other hand, how many times do I get to give my mom something that is one of one, that illustrates how unique she is and how much she means to me? Yes, I could do a lot of good with the money this bracelet cost. But this wasn't about wasting money, because I don't make this kind of purchase often. There was something incredibly meaningful for me to show my mother how special she is by giving her this lavish gift. It wasn't about the diamonds. It wasn't about how much it sparkled. It wasn't about how expensive it was. It was about the priceless moment of showing my mother that she was worth it. Yes, I bought it.

For a long time, I thought about what to write in the card. I finally landed on something like, "Mom, I love you so much. This is a one-of-one piece, just like you." I'll never forget giving this gift to her at Christmas. She opened the card first and was overcome with emotion. Her hands trembled and her eyes watered. When she unwrapped the box with the bracelet, she gasped. "I can't wear this, Timmy," she burst out, crying.

It took a few minutes for Mom to wrap her head around receiving such an extravagant gift. Later, she told me it reminded her of how extravagant God is with us. He loves us lavishly. He loves us more than we can imagine. We don't deserve it. And we can't earn it. We can only choose to accept His gift.

I haven't always been able to give my mom expensive things. But I've always given out of my heart, out of whatever I had to offer.

I remember when I was a young boy, Mom got terribly sick one Christmas Eve. She has an inner ear condition that causes her to suffer from extreme nausea and vertigo. That day and the next, Mom stayed in bed. She was so dizzy she couldn't even move her head from side to side. I can't even imagine how hard being bedridden was for Mom. For us, Christmas wasn't the same. Mom was the one who made this time of year special.

Seeing her so sick and unable to do everything she does to make Christmas happen broke my heart. But I knew something that might lift her spirits. Because of this inner ear condition, leaning over made Mom really dizzy, so much so that she couldn't weed the front yard landscape. By this time that year, the area was overgrown. This was one chore none of us kids enjoyed doing. I knew that Mom's love language is acts of service. With that in mind, I had a plan to give her the best gift ever.

On that cold and rainy Christmas Eve night, while everyone was asleep, I grabbed Dad's flashlight and snuck out my bedroom window. For hours, under pouring rain and guided only by flashlight, I pulled out every single weed. The sun was slowly rising as I tore out the last one from the soft earth.

I didn't know this at the time, but when she woke up Christmas morning, one of my siblings saw what I was doing and rushed to Mom's bedside to tell her. She was so happy. She couldn't get out of bed until the next day or two to see the tidy yard, but she told me it was one of her most precious moments.

My family spent Christmas Day that year gathered around Mom's bed. When it was time to open gifts, looking back, I'm pretty sure my present of weeding the front yard was even more meaningful than when I gave her that expensive bracelet many years later. But in both cases, it was about making the moment special for her.

Make It Count with Jesus

This is the day to make moments matter, with your loved ones or with strangers you may never meet again and whose day you can make brighter. More importantly, this is the day to make your life count with Jesus. If you have never done this before, I want to encourage you to accept the greatest gift of all, God's one and only Son.

The good news of Jesus is not a church-based product. It's a gift of hope, of eternal life. The God of this universe has bestowed on us a love greater than we can ever imagine. First John 3:1 says, "See what great love the Father has lavished on us, that we should be called children of God!" (NIV). That is what we are. Lavished! And through faith in Jesus, we are united to God.

God sent His Son, Jesus, on a rescue mission so you could live an abundant life. He loves you so much that if you were the only person on this planet, He would still send Jesus down to earth for you.

Jesus showed up and said, "I gotcha. I'm coming on a rescue mission for you because I love you. And no matter what you've done, it's not too bad. Wherever you are in this moment, you are not too lost. I love you. I came to save you." Jesus died on a cross for you. But that's not all—He didn't stay dead. He rose from the dead. Jesus defeated death, and He offers you life in Him. This is better than any extravagant gift I could ever give the ones I love.

Do you want to know the best part? You don't have to work for it! You can't earn this gift. You can never be good enough. You can never be rich enough. You can never work hard enough for it. It's not about what you can do to deserve this gift. It's about what Jesus did.

Have you accepted the free gift of a hope-filled life? Right now, as you read these words, you may feel convicted. You may feel a nudging of your heart. You may feel Jesus knocking on the door of your soul. Don't fight it.

Open the door. God is trying to speak to you. He is saying, "I love you. I want to live with you. I want to be part of your life. I want to make you My child. I want to bring you home."

When you make the decision to follow Jesus, to accept His gift of eternal life, your life is changed. You instantly go from darkness to light. You instantly become a child of God. You instantly have a home in heaven. And you instantly have God's presence, all the time. He will never leave you or forsake you. No matter what obstacles hit, He will be with you. No matter how hard things get, He will be there for you. No matter how lonely you feel, He will be by your side.

> Have you accepted the free gift of a hope-filled life?

God loves you. I love you. And this is your day! I want to give you the opportunity to do something life changing. If you'd like to make the decision to trust Jesus, I want to invite you to pray. You can use these words or pray in your own words:

Dear Jesus, I know I am a sinner and need a Savior. Thank You that You died on the cross for me and rose again. I open the door of my heart and ask You to come in. I trust only You, Jesus. Thank You for coming into my heart and forgiving my sins. Thank You that God is my Father and I am His child. Thank You that I have a home in heaven and that I will come and live with You someday. In Jesus's name, amen.

If you have just prayed this prayer, I want to welcome you into the family of God. You are now my brother or sister in Jesus Christ! I pray that the decision you just made makes this day the greatest in your life.

Each day we have offers meaning, purpose, and a chance to do something better, different, bigger. Today is a day to say "I love you." It's a day to get in the game. It's a day to stop living in the past. It's a day to listen to the right voice. It's a day to believe. It's a day to open your eyes and say yes. It's a day to work hard for something that matters. It's a day to live with open hands. It's a day to remember that God is bigger than any giant before you. It's a day to connect with Him and go back to the well. And it's a day to make every moment count.

We often promise ourselves that one day we're going to do this or do that. But we're not guaranteed *one* day. Who knows if it will even come?

Besides, life isn't just about *one* day. It's about *this* day.

Acknowledgments

Mom and Dad: Thank you for believing in me and always praying for me. One of the biggest honors in my life is to call you Mom and Dad. I love you.

Christy (a.k.a. Chri), Katie (a.k.a. Katz), Robby (a.k.a. Dobbs), and Peter (a.k.a. the Peter): The best times of my life have been with you guys. I hope each of you knows how special you are to me. I look forward to many more late-night sessions of laughing till we cry. Love you guys.

The TTF team: I'm so grateful for each and every one of you. Thanks for standing beside me and showing God's love as we fight to help those in need.

Annie (Green Gables): Thank you for always making sure all is well. You make it seem so easy!

Esther and Whitney at the Fedd Agency: Thank you for continuing to believe in me and for all the heart and effort you put into this project.

AJ: God truly gave you a gift. Thank you for lending your talents to my story and for always being willing to take my calls to talk about an idea, process a story, or laugh about life!

Tina, Bruce, Laura, Chris, Ginia, Bev, Lisa, Tammy, and Kristopher at WaterBrook: Thank you for championing this book with continued excellence and passion.

Brodie: You've been so much more than an agent; you've been a friend. Thank you for helping me on this journey. Here's to a lot of stories to come!

Marcus, Laura, and Paul of *SEC Nation:* This is more than a show; it's family. I'm grateful for you guys.

Wendy: What can I say? You're family.

About the Author

Tim Tebow is a two-time national college football champion, first-round NFL draft pick, and Heisman Trophy winner. After playing in the NFL for the Denver Broncos and the New York Jets, Tebow joined the SEC Network. In addition to his role on *SEC Nation,* the network's traveling road show, Tebow also contributes to a variety of other ESPN platforms. In 2016, he signed a professional baseball contract with the New York Mets. Through everything, Tim's true passion remains the work of the Tim Tebow Foundation, which he began in 2010. The foundation's mission is to bring Faith, Hope, and Love to those needing a brighter day in their darkest hour of need. The foundation is fulfilling that mission every day by serving thousands of deserving children around the world. Learn more at timtebow.com.

BRONCO AND FRIENDS

A Party to Remember

New York Times Bestselling Author

Tim Tebow

with A.J. Gregory   Illustrated by Jane Chapman

(spine) Tim Tebow · BRONCO AND FRIENDS · A Party to Remember · WATERBROOK

Bronco and his animal friends are invited to a party. When they encounter a series of obstacles, they discover how working as a team makes all the difference. Tim Tebow's delightful story, based on his own pup, illustrates for young readers that God sees every one of us as special, unique, and essential to the party.

Free coloring pages at
BroncoAndFriends.com!

TIM TEBOW
FOUNDATION™

FAITH • HOPE • LOVE

To continue to fight for those who can't fight for themselves, a portion of proceeds from each book sold will be donated to the **Tim Tebow Foundation** to help further their mission of:

Bringing Faith, Hope and Love to those needing a brighter day in their darkest hour of need.

The foundation is currently fulfilling this mission every day by...

- Providing life-changing surgeries through the **Tebow CURE Hospital** to children of the Philippines who could not otherwise afford care.

- Creating a worldwide movement through **Night to Shine**, an unforgettable prom experience, centered on God's love, for people with special needs.

- Building **Timmy's Playrooms** in children's hospitals around the world.

- Fulfilling the dreams of children with life-threatening illnesses through the **W15H** program.

- Encouraging volunteer service to others through **Team Tebow** and **Team Tebow Kids**.

- Supporting housing, meals, medical treatment and education for orphans around the world though our **Orphan Care** program.

- Providing **Adoption Aid** financial assistance to families who are making the courageous choice to adopt a child with special needs internationally.

...simply put, Serving Children and Sharing God's Love!

To learn more about these initiatives and the continued growth of the foundation's outreach ministries, visit **www.timtebowfoundation.org**.

New York Times Bestseller!

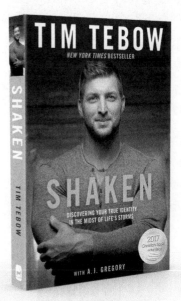

What defines your self-worth? Is it your successes or your failures? Former NFL quarterback and professional baseball outfielder Tim Tebow shares never-before-told details about his joys and disappointments on and off the field in *Shaken,* a *New York Times* bestseller and the Evangelical Christian Publishers Association 2017 Book of the Year. With captivating honesty, Tebow explains how his identity has remained steadfast and secure in God alone.

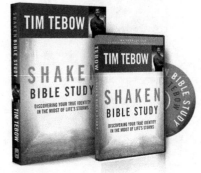

The Shaken Bible Study and DVD serve as additional resources and excellent companions to *Shaken.* These resources are ideally packaged for adult and youth small groups, student athletes, and mentorship programs, as well as individual study.

PERFECT FOR YOUNG READERS!

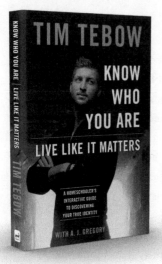

Tim Tebow encourages young people to tackle insecurity, stand out from the crowd, and develop an unshakeable identity based on God's standard—not the world's.

Tim Tebow describes the highs and the lows of his sports career and reminds young Christians that in a world driven by likes, the only opinion that truly matters is God's.

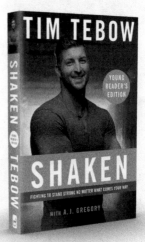